MIGRATION AND GLOBAL GOVERNANCE

KATIE WILLIS AND PAUL WRAIGHT
SERIES EDITORS: BOB DIGBY AND SUE WARN

© Geographical Association, 2020

This book is copyright under the Berne Convention. All rights are reserved. Apart from any fair dealing for the purpose of private study, research, criticism or review, as permitted under the Copyright, Designs and Patents Act 1988, no part of this publication may be reproduced, stored in a retrieval system, or transmitted in any form or by any means, electronic, electrical, chemical, mechanical, optical, photocopying, recording or otherwise, without the prior written permission of the copyright owner. Enquiries should be addressed to the Geographical Association. The authors have licensed the Geographical Association to allow members to reproduce material for their own internal school/departmental use, provided that the authors hold the copyright. The views expressed in this publication are those of the authors and do not necessarily represent those of the Geographical Association.

ISBN 978-1-84377-478-5
First published 2020
Impression number 10 9 8 7 6 5 4 3 2 1
Year 2022 2021 2020

Published by the Geographical Association, 160 Solly Street, Sheffield S1 4BF

The Geographical Association (GA) is the leading subject association for all teachers of geography. Our charitable mission is to further geographical knowledge and understanding through education. Our journals, publications, professional events, website and local and online networks support teachers and share their ideas and practice. The GA represents the views of geography teachers and plays a leading role in public debate relating to geography and education.

Company number 07139068
Registered charity: no 1135148
Website: www.geography.org.uk
E-mail: info@geography.org.uk

The GA would be happy to hear from other potential authors who have ideas for geography books. You may contact the Head of Publishing at the address above.

Cover image: © Lasse Simonen/Shutterstock.com

Copy edited by Fran Royle
Editorial production by Fran Royle
Cartography/illustrations by Kim Farrington
Designed and typeset by Ledgard Jepson Ltd
Printed and bound in the UK by W&G Baird

Disclaimer: Every effort has been made to identify and contact the original sources of copyright material. If there have been any inadvertent breaches of copyright we apologise.

Contents

Editors' preface	4
Chapter 1 Introduction	5
Chapter 2 Population and globalisation	7
Chapter 3 Migration classification and regulation	16
Chapter 4 The human experience of migration	23
Chapter 5 The consequences of migration	33
Chapter 6 The contested nature of migration	41
Chapter 7 The fluidity of borders	47
Key terms	51

Editors' preface

The *Top Spec Geography* series is designed to be used by 16–19 year olds in schools and colleges. The writing teams, combining the expertise of a specialist in their field with that of an experienced classroom teacher, have been chosen to ensure that contemporary and exciting geography, which brings together the latest research and thinking on topical themes, is accessible to post-16 students.

Each book in the series consists of:
- written chapters, with illustrations and data that complement the text
- activities for use in groups and as guides for private study. Some activities are designed to encourage discussion, while others help to promote students' understanding of the issues
- background theory, to enable students to see the wider picture
- key information boxes
- ideas for further research: most post-16 teaching encourages students to become independent learners and some specifications have research units designed to help students prepare for this.
- a glossary of key words and terms.

In addition, there are online resources that have been written to extend and complement the book, and will ensure that the most up-to-date research and data are available. Each chapter will remind you about these resources, which can be found at www.geography.org.uk/topspec. Although the books have been written mainly with geography students in mind, the series may also prove useful for students:
- taking public examination or diploma courses in other subjects such as environmental science
- who want to read beyond their exam courses in order to apply or prepare for university study
- studying new topics in their first year at university.

Migration and global governance

This book meets the requirements of the 2016 A levels in England and Wales. Its theme, migration and global governance, features in all four A level specifications, even though the specifications differ slightly in detail.

The book includes:
- migration as a response to demographics and economic development
- the structures of global governance that shape patterns of migration, such as border systems and visas, and movements of refugees between countries
- the theoretical background to migration, which seeks to explain the geography of different migrations (such as elite migration and rural to urban migration in developing economies)
- the consequences of migration for host and source countries, communities, households and individuals
- an examination, through concepts such as multiculturalism, nationalism and populism, of why migration can be highly contested
- how the human experience of migration varies and can change over time.

A level specifications require students to study the ways in which migrations affect places and people, and how political responses may vary from local to global. This book addresses these ideas through the liberal use of examples.

The book will help students who undertake individual investigations on migration as part of their A level. Chapters 6 and 7 will be particularly useful, providing context for studying the impacts of migration on places, and how the experience of migration may vary for different individuals and groups.

Bob Digby and Sue Warn
January 2020

Online resources

Each book in the *Top Spec Geography* series has a range of supplementary materials and resources including:
- extra information
- extended question lists
- model answers and mark schemes
- links to relevant websites
- extended glossaries
- photo galleries.

To access these go to **www.geography.org.uk/topspec** then click on the button for this book. You will then be asked for your password.

The unique password for this book is WW14T3

1. Introduction

This book will describe and explain the processes of migration at a range of scales, governed to varying extents by a variety of actors. It is a complex story, subject to interpretation that is developing over time as the factors driving migration change and the actors seeking to manage the processes adapt and respond to them.

Structure of the book
Chapter 2 will examine how demographics and economic development create a context for the geography of migration. Chapter 3 will look at the structures of global governance that shape patterns of migration. Chapter 4 will introduce models that aim to explain migration and the geography of different migrations:
- elite migration
- rural to urban migration in developing economies
- south-south migration
- regular and irregular international migration.

Chapter 5 will explore the consequences of migration for host and source countries, communities, households and individuals. Chapter 6 will consider why migration is often contested, exploring ideas such as multiculturalism, transnationalism, nationalism and populism. Finally, in Chapter 7, the book will explore the fluidity of borders and how the human experience of migration cannot be easily categorised. The experience of different groups varies and can change over time.

Relevant terminology will be defined in each chapter or in the Key terms. We have adopted the United Nations Human Development Index (HDI), a measure of life expectancy, education and per capita income, to compare countries (see Information Box 1.1).

INFORMATION BOX 1.1 HUMAN DEVELOPMENT INDEX (HDI)

HDI is expressed as a value from 1 to 0 (values above 0.8 are very high, values below 0.55 are low) or as a rank (ordering countries from 1 to 188, where 1 is the country with the highest level of human development). To understand complex patterns of migration it is necessary to move beyond the simple more, or less, economically developed country (MEDC/LEDC) categorisation: HDI is more meaningful in terms of people's life expectancy, education and income. The UN also constructs four HDI groupings – Very High; High; Medium; and Low – that better reflect the distinctions between countries in our complex world. These differences are important to understand this story of migration and global governance.

Figure 1.1 Border patrol car on the US side of the USA-Mexico border. **Photo:** © Manuela Durson/Shutterstock.

Migration and global governance are complex
The title of this book could be thought to suggest that migration is a readily defined process, governed by established rules at the global scale. The reality of migration is very different. Migrations are hard to define. They occur over different scales in terms of space, time and magnitude. They can be contested or welcomed by both host and source societies. Moreover, these attitudes can change over time as well.

Equally, 'global governance' might imply that there are institutions with the authority and capacity to manage migration at the global scale, but the reality is also very different. Migration is governed by a patchwork of laws, institutions and norms. Some apply at the global scale. In practice, most are applied regionally and nationally. Authority to manage migration is dispersed between intergovernmental organisations, at the global and regional scale, and national governments. In some countries, local authorities have a significant role to play. Non-governmental organisations (NGOs) can also have varying amounts of influence at different scales and times.

Therefore the governance of migration varies in its extent and effectiveness. Many migrations occur despite global governance, in ungoverned spaces, in periods of crisis and chaos. This connects migration to the geographies of organised crime, people trafficking, modern-day slavery, conflict and failed states. Moreover, the context in which migrations occur has a significant influence on the extent to which they are welcomed or resisted.

Why are migration and global governance so complex?

The experience of the Second World War (1939–1945), and the desire to prevent another such conflict, motivated many countries to seek a way of mitigating the problems that drove the world towards conflict in the 1930s: nationalism, economic depression, and an absence of national self-determination.

In 1945 the United Nations (UN) was founded by 51 countries committed to maintaining international peace. The UN's founding charter stated its purposes, among others, as:
- *to save succeeding generations from the scourge of war, which twice in our lifetime has brought untold sorrow to mankind*
- *to reaffirm faith in fundamental human rights, in the dignity and worth of the human person, the equal rights of men and women and of nations large and small*
- *to establish conditions under which justice and respect for the obligations arising from treaties and other sources of international law can be maintained.* (UN, 1945)

The institutions and policies of the UN regarding migration are set out in Chapter 2.

The spirit of international co-operation and the ideal of human rights that motivated the UN's founders is clear. Why were they unable to establish the global governance needed to put these principles fully into practice?

Firstly, within a decade the Second World War transitioned into the Cold War. The capitalist West, led by the USA, and the communist Eastern bloc, headed by the USSR (and later China) may both have espoused a similar rhetoric of human rights. However, their economic and political systems were not compatible, leading to conflict rather than co-operation in many of the intergovernmental institutions of the post-war world.

Secondly, independence movements dismantled the European empires that had dominated much of the pre-war world. Both the USA, which in the 18th century fought its own War of Independence against the British, and the communist Eastern bloc, which regarded empire as a form of oppression, supported the process of decolonisation. Countries previously united under imperial rule split up into independent nations. The capitalist West and the communist Eastern bloc vied for influence in these newly independent nations, in some cases conducting 'proxy wars', as in Vietnam. More nations, more borders; all contributed to an increasingly complicated context for global governance. In 1945 the UN General Assembly had 51 member states. By 2018 it had 193. It is much harder to reach consensus and agree policies as a result.

Some former colonies, for instance Singapore and the Gulf States, have successful economies and are major host nations for migrants. Less economically successful independent nations, for instance Nepal and Nigeria, have become major source nations for migration.

The Cold War ended in the early 1990s. Economic globalisation, led by the USA and enthusiastically supported by other nations in the Organisation for Economic Co-operation and Development (OECD) and emerging economies, has caused significant demographic and economic changes. More people want to migrate; the economic incentives for them to do so are even stronger; but the barriers to effective global governance of migration have not gone away – not least, the rise in economic protectionism that followed the 2008 financial crisis. Proxy wars in the Syrian Arab Republic and Yemen are creating tensions amongst regional powers in the Middle East. The emerging trade war between the USA and China could further limit multilateral co-operation. Brexit and rising nationalism in the European Union is another reason to be concerned about the future of international co-operation.

Therefore, the complexity of migration and global governance is a product of the piecemeal way the governance of migration has emerged since the Second World War, and the way in which subsequent wars and crises have been resolved. It is also because national governments, seeking to preserve their autonomy, have sometimes resisted international co-operation. More fundamentally, it is the story of the myriad ways human beings have sought to better their lives and escape hardship and tyranny in the gaps between the theory and practice of global governance.

Reference
UN (1945) *Charter of the United Nations.* Available at https://tinyurl.com/jz46kyv (last accessed 1/10/2019).

2. Population and globalisation

In May 2019 the UN estimated the population of the world at 7.7 billion, and it is continuing to grow. According to the UN the most likely scenario, within a range of 7.3 to 10.7 billion, is that world population will reach 8.5 billion by 2030 and 9.7 billion by 2050 (UN Department of Economic and Social Affairs Population Division (UN DESA), 2019). Within the next 30 years, therefore, it is reasonable to expect an increase in global population of about 25%.

Such strong overall population growth is a relatively modern phenomenon. The UN has estimated that it took 200,000 years for world population to grow to 1 billion, but only a further 200 years to reach 7 billion, in 2011 (UN DESA, 2017) (see Figure 2.1). This is because prior to the Industrial Revolution (roughly 1750–1850) death rates from disease, poor diet and wars meant that parents were rarely survived by more than two of their children. Families were large, but mortality rates were also high. Birth rates balanced death rates, leaving population sizes relatively stable.

Populations grow when the birth rate (the number of births per 1000 people) exceeds the death rate (the number of deaths per 1000 people). As societies became wealthier and more scientifically advanced, sanitation, housing, diet and education began to improve. Death rates began to slow relative to birth rates and the long expansion of human population began. In very high HDI economies, rising prosperity after the Second World War and the gradual introduction of welfare states accelerated this process. In lower HDI economies, the affluence and technologies to support a declining birth rate are more recent, but the impact is the same.

There is no great secret behind our fast-growing world population. It is not the case that a few people are having very large families; rather, that the world's population is made up of more young people than old people. There are more people in their childbearing and child-raising years, compared to those beyond their fertile years: in this context population is bound to increase. Nevertheless, you may have noticed in Figure 2.1 that the rate of population increase has declined since 1968. This is because an increasing proportion of the world's population is getting old, which will gradually reduce the expected number of births relative to deaths.

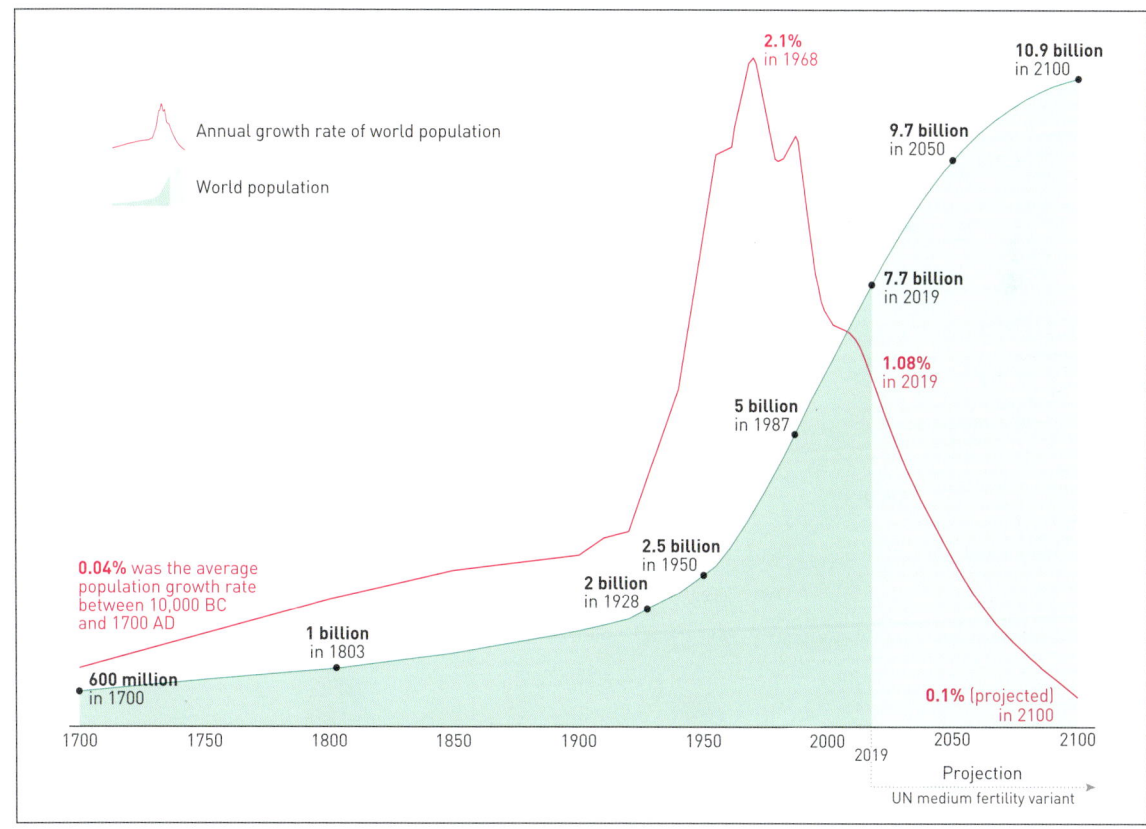

Figure 2.1 World population growth, 1700–2100 (projected). **Data sources:** Our World in Data based on HYDE, UN, and UN Population Division (2019 revision), licensed under CC-BY by the author Max Roser.

This process is shown by the demographic transition model (Figure 2.3).

The demographic transition model

The demographic transition model is a description, based on historical population trends, of the changing patterns of mortality, fertility and growth rates that influence population size. Although the model has defined stages, these are theoretical. In reality the examples are in flux, so can be difficult to fit to precise stages. Currently there are no countries at stage 1 of the model.

Stage 1

Before the Industrial Revolution, birth and death rates were both high, so population sizes were low and fairly stable. This corresponds to stage 1 of the model. At this stage the population pyramid is very wide at the base and very narrow at the top.

Figure 2.2 Young people in Manila, 2012. With a median age of 24.1, and just 4% of its citizens aged over 65, the Philippines has a very youthful population. **Photo:** © Rey Borlaza/Shutterstock.

INFORMATION BOX 2.1 POPULATION PYRAMID

A population pyramid shows the distribution of various age groups in a population. They are called pyramids because the graph shows a pyramid shape when the population is growing due to natural increase. Males and females are indicated separately, so the graph shows if there is an unequal distribution of the sexes in a given age group. When the population of a country is youthful the graph will be broader at the base. When a country has an older population the graph will be narrow at the base and broader as age increases.

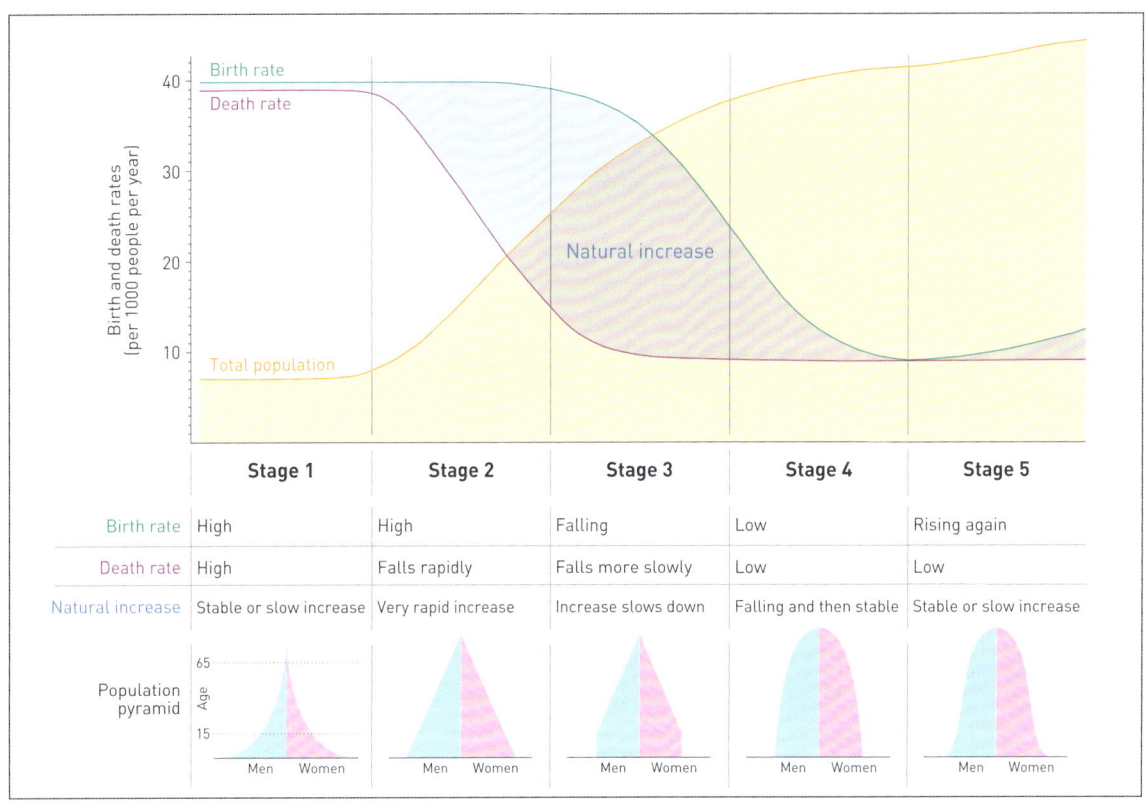

Figure 2.3 The demographic transition model. **Source:** Our World in Data. The author Max Roser licensed this visualisation under a CC BY-SA license.

Stage 2

With better health and declining infant mortality, death rates fall and populations grow rapidly. This is stage 2 of the model. Countries at this stage in the model have a regular-shaped pyramid.

A few countries are still in the early stages of the model. They have a very youthful population but also a high death rate, due to poor diet and sanitation, conflict or limited access to healthcare, although in a globalised world very few places are beyond the reach of international aid organisations. Such countries are at stage 2/stage 3. In Eritrea, eastern Africa, for example, the median age is only 18.9 years. As few as 3% of its 5.7 million citizens are over 65, whereas a very significant 14% are under 5. Its population pyramid is very broad among the 0–4 years band. Every later band is significantly smaller, creating the textbook pyramid shape of a fast growing population. The pyramid tapers at the 20–24 band and again at 40–44. However, Eritrea's population growth rate, at 1.4%, is slower than might be expected. This is much faster than countries like the USA, which has a growth rate of 0.6%. However, it is much slower than countries with similar low HDI levels such as Ethiopia, also in eastern Africa, which has a population growth rate of 2.6% (World Bank Data Bank, 2019a).

Stage 3

With improved economic conditions and access to contraception, birth rates fall, and death rates also fall, though more slowly. Population growth continues, but at a lower rate. Stage 3 describes most middle HDI, and some high HDI, countries.

Some countries have only recently begun to transition into stages 2 and 3 of the model. They have a large population, and a fast growth rate relative to countries at stage 4; however it is likely to slow over time. The population remains very youthful and the conditions that ensure a long and healthy life are only slowly taking hold. In the Philippines in Southeast Asia, for example, the median age is 24.1 years. Just 4% of its 106.8 million citizens are over 65, whereas a sizeable 11% are under the age of 5 (UN Development Programme (UNDP), 2019). Its population pyramid is broadest among the 0–5 years band. Every later band is slightly smaller, creating the textbook pyramid shape of a fast growing population. The pyramid tapers quickly from middle age and there are very few people in the most elderly bands.

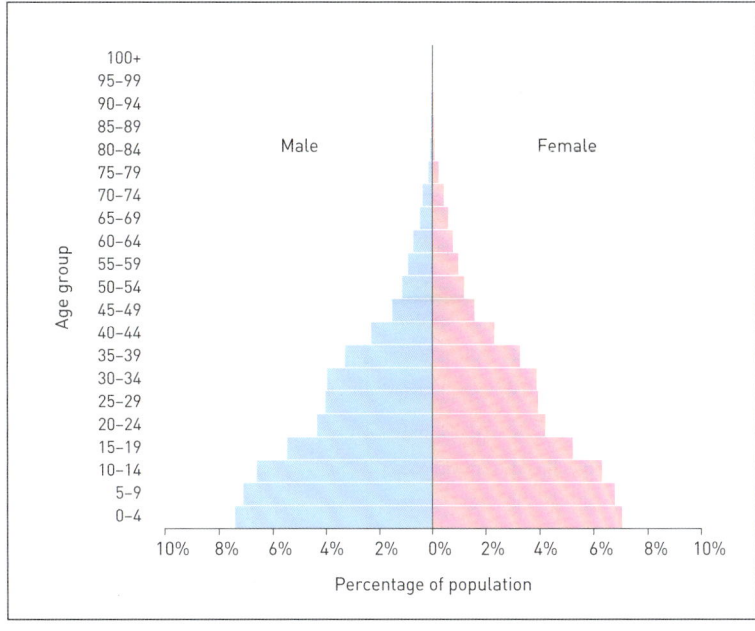

Figure 2.4 Population pyramid for Eritrea (population 5,753,934 in 2019). **Source:** World Bank populationpyramid.net, licensed under CC-BY 4.0.

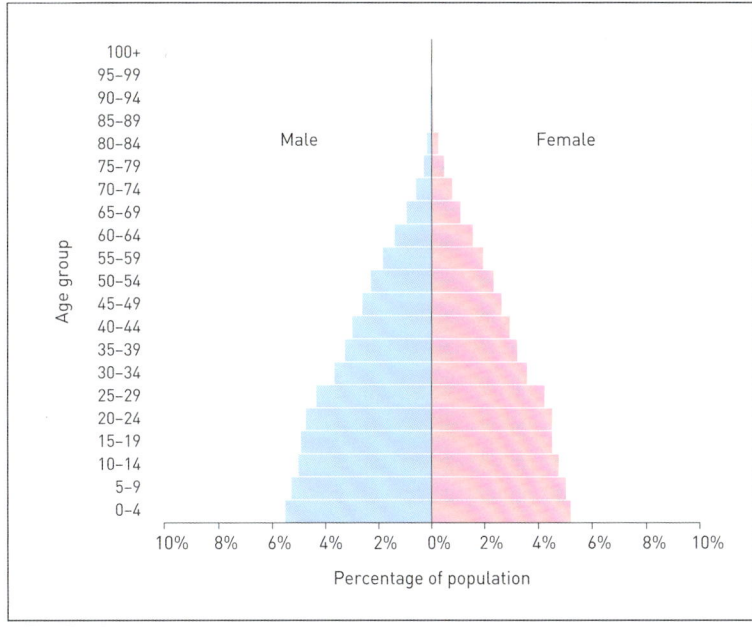

Figure 2.5 Population pyramid for the Philippines (population 106,886,636 in 2019). **Source:** World Bank populationpyramid.net, licensed under CC-BY 4.0.

Stage 4

In countries with strong economies and good healthcare and education, the population is stable, with a fertility rate of about two children per woman. Most very high HDI countries are at stage 4 of the model.

Countries that began their progress through the model a little earlier now have a large population. It is perhaps still growing, but at a much slower rate. They would have had a very youthful population in recent memory and the growth of a more elderly population is only just starting. In Mexico in North America, for example, the median age is 27.5 years and 7% of its 133.3 million citizens are over 65, whereas 9% are under the age of 5 (UNDP, 2019). Its population pyramid is broadest among the youthful age bands; however the youngest bands are narrower than the 15–19 and 20–24 bands. The pyramid tapers quickly after later middle age and there are few people in the most elderly bands.

Countries that industrialised early moved through the stages of the model first. As a result, they have a large population but their growth rate is now slow, or even in decline. Their population would have been very youthful at the start of their progress through the model, but has become increasingly elderly. In the USA, for example, the median age is 37.6 years. 15.4% of its 331.1 million citizens are over 65 and only 6% are under 5 (UNDP, 2019). Its population pyramid is narrower in the youthful bands than in the middle-aged bands. It is broadest in the 25–29 and 55–59 bands. It also has a significant number of people in the most elderly bands.

Stage 5

Theoretically, if a country's birth rate declines to the point where it is lower than the death rate, and the population could start to fall, that country would be at stage 5 of the demographic transition model.

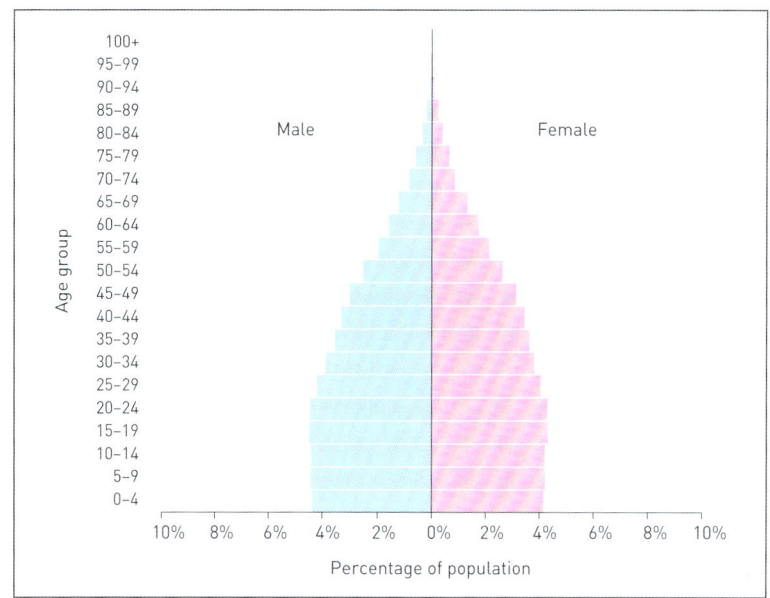

Figure 2.6 Population pyramid for Mexico (population 133,326,827 in 2019).
Source: World Bank populationpyramid.net, licensed under CC-BY 4.0.

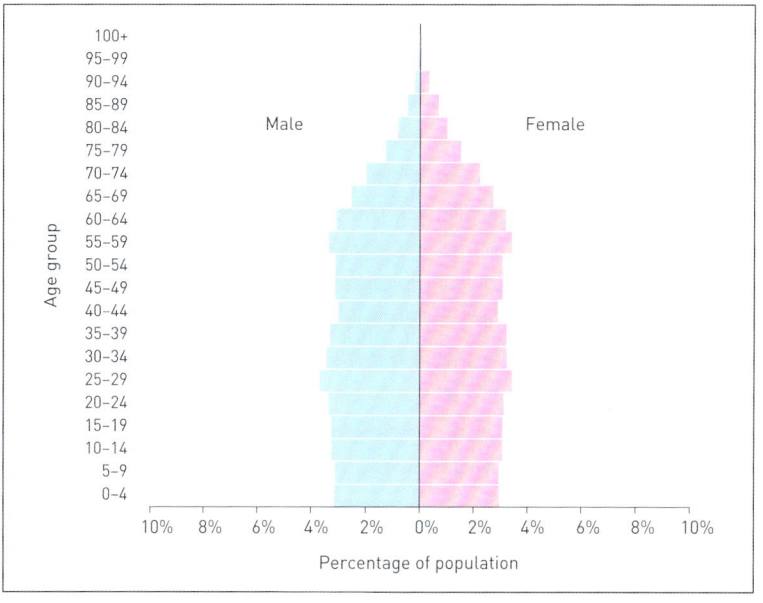

Figure 2.7 Population pyramid for the USA (population 331,195,364 in 2019).
Source: World Bank populationpyramid.net, licensed under CC-BY 4.0.

What is the impact of demographics on migration?

So far, we have seen how the demographic transition model explains our rising world population. However, the principles of the model are also very significant in explaining patterns of migration, because different countries are at different stages of the model at different times.

The structure of a country's population creates a context that begins to explain the factors influencing patterns of migration. Countries in stages 4 and 5 have an ageing population. Retired people may well have significant disposable income and therefore create high demand for labour in service industries. In 2017 services accounted for 80% of the US economy, but less than 60% of the Filipino and Eritrean economies (CIA, 2019). An ageing population also experiences worsening health, which creates increased demand for health and care services. The working age population has to pay through taxation for state provision of the services needed by the retired population.

Different dependency ratios

Different countries have markedly different dependency ratios. The USA has an old age dependency ratio of 23.5, higher than Mexico's of 10.3, the Philippines' of 7.6 and Eritrea's of 6.6 (UNDP, 2019). These factors create the conditions for migration into the USA. Workers are required for the health, social care and service industries to meet the needs of the USA's ageing population. In 2017 health expenditure in the USA accounted for 17.1% of the gross domestic product (GDP), compared with 4.7% in the Philippines and 3.3% in Eritrea (CIA, 2019). The American insurance-based healthcare system is another reason why health spending comprises such a high proportion of GDP. Workers cannot easily be found domestically because of the declining proportion of the population entering the workforce each year. Furthermore, the influx of migrant workers will swell the ranks of the tax-paying population, reducing the burden on the state of funding provision for the elderly.

Countries that are in the earlier stages of the demographic transition model have a different context for migration. They are experiencing faster population growth, and every year more children reach working age. This demographic dividend drives the domestic economy. However, the surplus of workers holds down wages by creating competition for each job, causing the standard of living to rise slowly if at all. Again, the differences between countries can be quite stark: Eritrea has a young age dependency ratio of 76.5, higher than the Philippines' of 50, Mexico's of 40.1 and the USA's of 28.8 (UNDP, 2019).

Figure 2.8 A busy zebra crossing in the Zócalo, Mexico City. With a median age of 27.5 and 7% of its 133.3 million citizens over 65, the growth of Mexico's elderly population is only just starting. **Photo:** © Aleksandar Todorovic/Shutterstock.

Figure 2.9 Senior citizens in Little Havana, Miami, Florida, 2018. In the USA the median age is 37.6 and 15.4% of its citizens are over 65. **Photo:** © Fotoluminate LLC/Shutterstock.

INFORMATION BOX 2.2 DEPENDENCY RATIO

The dependency ratio compares the non-working age population (aged 0–14 and 65+) to the working age population (aged 15–64). The formula is expressed thus:

$$\text{dependency ratio} = \frac{\text{young dependents} + \text{old dependents}}{\text{working age population}} \times 100$$

If the school leaving age or the retirement age changes, so does the ratio. A low ratio means there is a large working, tax-paying population to support children and retired people. A high ratio indicates greater pressure on the working population to fund services for the non-working population. This ratio can be broken down into the **old age dependency ratio** (ratio of the population aged 65 and above to the population aged 15–64) and the **young age dependency ratio** (ratio of the population aged 0–14 to the population aged 15–64).

A large pool of labour creates the conditions in which migration to countries or regions with a shrinking working age population becomes attractive. Wage differentials can be significant and there may be more opportunities for career progression. The advantages for the source countries of permitting out-migration are also clear: a large, youthful, under-employed population fuels the grey and black ('shadow') economy and can be a source of disorder and rioting. Migration can reduce these pressures; it has the added benefit of remittances to support the migrants' families. Moreover, returning migrants bring with them skills and connections that can support the domestic economy.

Globalisation and unequal levels of development

The International Monetary Fund (IMF) has described globalisation as

'the growing economic interdependence of countries worldwide through increasing volume and variety of cross-border transactions in goods and services, freer international capital flows, and more rapid and widespread diffusion of technology.'
(IMF, 1977, p. 45)

Thus globalisation is a process that develops over time as a result of government action and economic and technological change. As such, its impact on migration evolves over time. In particular, foreign direct investment (FDI) around the world changes the location of economic activity, which creates incentives for people to migrate.

The cumulative impact of patterns of FDI results in the rise of global networks that cross national boundaries. Networks create connections, and connections bring a range of advantages. For example, New York is a global financial centre: it hosts the headquarters of 24 Global 500 companies (the top 500 companies worldwide as measured by revenue) and is the headquarters of the United Nations. The city is switched on to globalisation and has benefited greatly as a result.

In 2019, in a city of 8.6 million people, nearly 1 million had a fortune of between US$1 million and US$30 million. Nearly 9000 had a fortune greater than US$30 million – the highest number of millionaires in any city in the world. Tokyo in Japan was in second place with just shy of 600,000 millionaires (Wealth X, 2019). The same networks that underpin this wealth reinforce patterns of migration. 37% of New York City's population are migrants. 19th century migration produced a city predominantly European in origin; the migration flows of the later 20th and early 21st centuries mean it now has no dominant ethnic group (Semple, 2013).

As shown in Figure 2.11, the world economy can be divided into three broad economic regions – core economies, semi-periphery economies and periphery economies – a simplification that helps us understand how economic geography creates a context for migration. This pattern changes over time and is not the definitive pattern of the global economy.

INFORMATION BOX 2.3 THE DEMOGRAPHIC DIVIDEND

The demographic dividend, as defined by the United Nations Population Fund, is 'the economic growth potential that can result from shifts in a population's age structure, mainly when the share of the working-age population is larger than the non-working-age share of the population' (UN Fund for Population Activities (UNFPA), (n.d.).)

INFORMATION BOX 2.4 THE SHADOW ECONOMY

The shadow economy includes all economic activities which are hidden from official authorities for monetary, regulatory, and institutional reasons. Monetary reasons include avoiding paying taxes and all social security contributions, regulatory reasons include avoiding governmental bureaucracy or the burden of regulatory framework, while institutional reasons include corruption law, the quality of political institutions and weak rule of law. Medina and Schneider, (2018, p. 4).

INFORMATION BOX 2.5 REMITTANCES

A remittance is a money transfer; in this context it refers to money sent by a migrant worker to someone in their home country. Remittances compete with international aid as one of the largest financial inflows to developing countries. In 2018, overall global remittances grew 10% to US$689 billion, of which US$528 billion went to developing countries. India receives the greatest annual amount, with US$79 billion in 2018. Other countries receiving large amounts in 2018 included the Philippines (US$34 billion) and Mexico (US$35 billion) (World Bank, 2019b).

MIGRATION AND GLOBAL GOVERNANCE

Figure 2.10 New York Stock Exchange: the trading floor. **Photo:** © Bart Sadowski/Shutterstock.

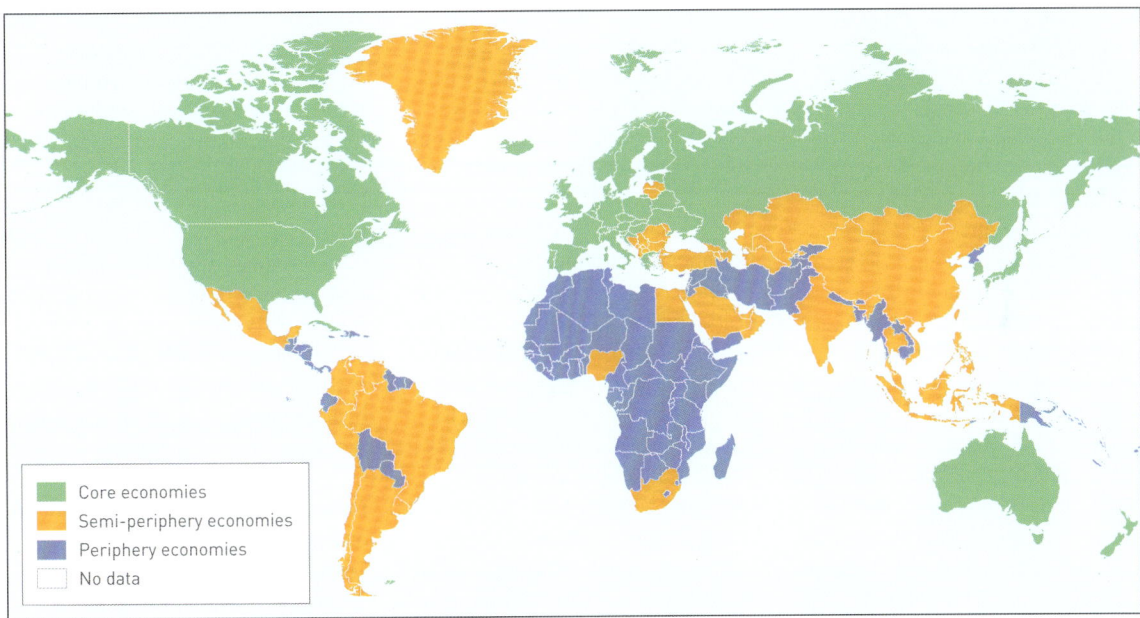

Figure 2.11 Globalisation and global economic regions. Adapted from Sheppard et al. (2009) and Dicken (2015). Republished with permission of Guilford Publications, Inc., permission conveyed through Copyright Clearance Center, Inc.

Core economies

These economies are highly urbanised and have 'very high' and 'high' HDI scores. They are characterised by greater social equality, high welfare provision and a large middle class. Their economies are dominated by service industries, satisfying their populations' high levels of consumption. They also have smaller high value-added manufacturing industries. Such states are very active in intergovernmental organisations (IGOs) such as the UN, OECD and World Trade Organization (WTO), so they also exert significant diplomatic influence. Core economies have benefited most from globalisation.

For example, the USA has a very high HDI value of 0.924, which is rank 13 in the world (UNDP, 2019). It is highly globalised, having received US$4 trillion of FDI from other countries and has invested US$6 trillion of FDI abroad. 80% of the economy is based on service/tertiary industries and less than 1% of the population work in low-wage agriculture. However in social and economic terms the USA is less equal than most core economies. Unusually for a core economy, 15% of the population exists below the poverty line, and the richest 10% own 30% of the nation's wealth (CIA, 2019).

Semi-periphery economies

Semi-periphery economies have been developing quickly in recent decades due to globalisation. They have not been accumulating wealth and capital for as long as core economies so have medium HDI values. They are urbanising rapidly and recently have seen rapid GDP growth. However, the speed of growth has led to great inequality, both spatially and socially. Although still significant, their primary industries are reducing in importance compared to their secondary industries. They tend to have limited tertiary and quaternary industries, but these are developing alongside their participation in IGOs.

Mexico and the Philippines are examples of semi-periphery economies. Mexico has a high HDI value of 0.774, which is rank 74 in the world (UNDP, 2019). It has been significantly incorporated into the global economy, having received US$554 billion of FDI and invested US$243 billion of FDI abroad. 64% of the economy is based on service industries and 13% of the population work in agriculture. In this very unequal society, where the richest 10% own 40% of the wealth, 46% of the population exists below the poverty line (CIA, 2019). The Philippines has a medium HDI score of 0.699, which is rank 113 in the world (UNDP, 2019). It is less involved in global financial flows than Mexico, having received US$79 billion of FDI and invested US$48 billion of FDI abroad. Only 60% of the economy is based on service industries and a significant 26% of the population work in agriculture. It is also a very unequal society; the richest 10% own 30% of the wealth and 21% live below the poverty line (CIA, 2019).

Figure 2.12 August 2019: Brand ambassadors distribute souvenir fans for the launch of Kura Sushi USA on the NASDAQ stock market. **Photo:** © rblfmr/Shutterstock.

Periphery economies

These economies tend to have low or low-middle HDI values. They have not benefitted from globalisation – not just because they lack global connections, but also because in many cases a colonial past has left a toxic legacy of ethnic conflict, contested borders and disadvantageous terms of trade that hinder economic growth. As a result, some periphery economies are considered failed states: a weak or divided government cannot provide the civil order necessary for a high quality of life for its people and meaningful participation in global networks. In these economies, the majority of the population live in rural areas (although primary cities may be urbanising fast). They rely on primary industries (regional agriculture may be subsistence-based), although some have important extractive industries. Poor governance leaves such industries vulnerable to asset grabs by elites, whose members syphon off revenues to tax havens, further hindering economic growth. Such states are rarely active in IGOs, although they will be members of the UN.

Eritrea has a low HDI score of 0.44, which is rank 179 in the world (UNDP, 2019). It is switched off from globalisation with negligible FDI. 80% of the population work in agriculture, of whom more than 50% live below the poverty line (CIA, 2019).

Demographic change, globalisation and migration

Demographic change creates a context of population surplus and deficit, but alone is insufficient to understand patterns of migration. It is globalisation that creates the push and pull factors driving migration in this context: we could describe globalisation both as the global growth in economic activity that has lifted billions out of poverty and as the global growth in economic activity that has produced a two-speed world. By creating unequal rates of growth in different places, globalisation drives rural to urban migration (in low and middle HDI economies) and international migration (in increasingly middle and some HDI economies). Chapter 3 will describe the complex legal barriers that constrain and channel migration. Chapter 4 will explore the models that geographers use to explain these processes in detail. However, it is worthwhile to finish this chapter by looking at how demographics and economic globalisation combine to create migration pressures for the USA, Mexico, the Philippines and Eritrea.

The USA has a heavy demand for both high- and low-skilled labour. It is highly globalised; the staff of its multinational companies must migrate to manage FDI at home and abroad; its scientists and academics work in globally connected universities and research industries; celebrities and the wealthy network in global cities and consume high-end goods and services. Moreover, its ageing population does not provide sufficient labour for agricultural jobs and labour-intensive service industries. Therefore, there is also a requirement for both seasonal and longer-term low-skilled migration.

Mexico's economy is also globalised, so also benefits from skilled migration, particularly within the manufacturing industries of the North American Free Trade Area (NAFTA). It has global cities, such as Mexico City, and an tourism industry, both of which encourage immigration. However, its youthful population, high rate of poverty, and proximity to and globalised links with the core economy of the USA provide significant incentives for emigration.

The Philippines has less high-skilled immigration than Mexico, but for similar reasons: executives to manage FDI, global cities such as Manila and a developed tourism industry. It has an even more youthful population, although slightly fewer live below the poverty line. This demographic and economic context, allied to strong post-Second World War links with the USA and long-established relationships within the Association of Southeast Asian Nations (ASEAN), provide a powerful impetus to migrate.

Eritrea is so switched off from globalisation that it has negligible in-migration. The capital, Asmara, has weak global connections and tourism is little developed. Eritrea has the most youthful population, and the highest rates of poverty, of all the four countries we have looked at. The demographic and economic incentives to migrate are very high; however, an authoritarian regime means the barriers to migration are also very high. It has some historical links to Italy, which colonised parts of north-east Africa. It also has some regional links to the United Arab Emirates (UAE), but broadly speaking it has only weak links to the global economy.

References

CIA (2019) *The World Factbook Country Profiles*. Available at https://tinyurl.com/y3hurcgs (last accessed 24/8/2019).

Dicken, P. (2015) *Global Shift* (7th edition). London: Guilford Press.

IMF (1997) *World Economic Outlook*. Washington, DC: IMF.

Medina, L. and Schneider, F. (2018) 'Shadow economies around the world: what did we learn over the last 20 years?' IMF Working Paper WP/18/17. Washington, DC: IMF.

Semple, K. (2013) 'Immigration remakes and sustains New York, report finds', *New York Times*, 18 December. Available at https://tinyurl.com/lycleey (last accessed 26/8/2019).

Sheppard, E., Porter, P.W., Faust, D.R. and Nagar, R. (2009) *A World of Difference: Encountering and Contesting Development* (2nd edition). New York: Guilford Press.

UN DESA (2019) 'World Population Prospects 2019: Highlights'. Available at https://tinyurl.com/y2u2a324 (last accessed 4/11/2019).

UNDP (2019) 'Human Development Reports'. Available at https://tinyurl.com/o66wese (last accessed 20/8/2019).

UNFPA (n.d.) 'Demographic dividend'. Available at https://tinyurl.com/yxq4p4km (last accessed 1/10/2019).

Wealth X (2019) *High Net Worth Handbook*, New York, NY, London and Dubai. Wealth X.

World Bank Data Bank (2019a) *Population Growth (Annual %)*. Available at https://tinyurl.com/ybzd2jbt (last accessed 26/8/2019).

World Bank Data Bank (2019b) *Personal remittances, received (current US$)*. Available at https://tinyurl.com/yym5b3bg (last accessed 26/8/2019).

ACTIVITY BOX 2

1. Research the population pyramid for your country of residence.
2. Using Figure 2.3, estimate your country's stage in the demographic transition model.
3a. Draw a spider diagram of the factors influencing the age distribution of any given country's population.
3b. Draw a spider diagram of the factors influencing the extent to which a country is connected to the global economy.
3c. Find connections between the factors in both spider diagrams.
4. Assess the importance of the population factors and economic factors that influence the incentives for migration, taking into account the connections between the spider diagrams.

Extra resources to accompany this chapter are available on the Top Spec web pages. See page 4 for further information.

3. Migration classification and regulation

Figure 3.1 Passengers queue at immigration control at Suvarnabhumi International Airport, Bangkok, Thailand.
Photo: © 1000 Words/Shutterstock.

Introduction

The governance of migration includes both classification and regulation. Governance can be defined as 'Forms of rule-making which encompass government and non-government actors such as private companies and civil society organizations' (Williams et al., 2014, p. 355). It can operate at a range of scales, from individual workplaces or organisations, municipal or national government, transnational corporations and regional trading blocs, to the global scale. This chapter describes how forms of migration have been classified at a global scale and what this means for its regulation. Despite the focus on global governance, a key argument in this chapter is that the implementation of global rules is conducted at a range of scales, leading to a diversity of laws and policies (Willis, 2018).

Definitions and statistics

The International Organization for Migration (IOM) (2017) uses the 1998 UN Recommendations on Statistics of International Migration as the basis for its reporting (see Information Box 3.1).

However, while the UN recommends the use of these definitions, there are no mechanisms to enforce them in national statistical reporting. Additionally, governments, members of host countries and migrants themselves may use the terms differently. It is important, therefore, to clarify what definitions are used in specific contexts when interpreting data.

Border control and the state

The UN is a very important institution in present-day global governance. However, its ability to achieve its goals is based on the agreement of individual states, and there is a potential tension between the ambitions of individual countries and the UN's wider global agenda. Article 2, Principle 7 of the 1945 UN Charter states

> 'Nothing contained in the present Charter shall authorize the United Nations to intervene in matters which are essentially within the domestic jurisdiction of any state:' (UN, 1945).

This recognises the sovereignty of individual states, which is key to the maintenance of the state system. David Storey (2017, p. 116) defines sovereignty as 'the authority of a state to rule over its territory and the people within its borders, without external interference'. An acceptance of sovereignty dates from the 1648 Treaty of Westphalia, which brought an end to a series of wars in western Europe.

Sovereign states have the right to control their borders, particularly who comes in and on what basis. Some states may also control who can leave the country. By controlling their borders states are acting to ensure their citizens' safety. Citizenship of a country will also come with particular rights, such as voting, access to education and some forms of healthcare, that are not always available to non-citizens, including migrants who are allowed entry.

Visa systems

No country in the world allows completely free movement across its borders. They all have immigration rules, implemented through a visa system. Each country's visa system will vary, but most will have visas that relate to employment, marriage, tourism and education. In some countries visas will allow for family reunification; there may also be a separate system to encourage immigration of entrepreneurs and investors, who are seen as bringing economic benefits to the country. Figure 3.2 provides a summary of the over 200 visa types available for entering legally into the USA.

Employment visas usually distinguish between different sectors of the economy, or levels of skill. This is so governments can bring in employees to fill shortage areas, so complementing the domestic labour force. The rights of labour migrants may vary depending on the nature of their employment. For example, the Singapore labour immigration system differentiates between professionals/skilled individuals, and those who are semi-skilled. The distinction is sometimes made between 'foreign workers' and 'foreign talent' (Ho, 2006). 'Foreign workers' are semi-skilled migrants, usually from other Asian countries, needed for construction work or domestic service. Under Singapore's visa system they will be granted a two-year work permit, after which they will have to return to their country of origin. They are not allowed to

---

INFORMATION BOX 3.1 MIGRATION

The IOM defines an international migrant as 'any person who changes his or her country of usual residence' (IOM, 2017, p. 299). This definition excludes people who are moving for reasons such as religious pilgrimage, a holiday, business or medical treatment. It also distinguishes between a long-term migrant, 'who moves to a country other than that of his or her usual residence for a period of at least a year (12 months), so that the country of destination effectively becomes his or her new country of usual residence', and a short-term migrant, whose move to a different country is for at least three months, but less than 12 (IOM, 2017, p. 299). Migration can be over short or long distances. Migration across domestic and international borders requires moving to a new political and legal regime. It is also possible to migrate within a region, staying within the same political and legal order. As a result, the scale of upheaval and nature of the obstacles to be overcome vary greatly between different forms of migration.

Selected non-immigrant visa categories (84 different visas)	Immigrant visa categories (132 different visas)
Athlete competing for prize money	Immediate relative and family-sponsored
Artist and entertainer	Employer-sponsored (plus spouse/children)
Business visitor	Immigrant investor (plus spouse/children)
Diplomat (plus spouse/children)	Diversity immigrant visa (plus spouse/children)
Airline and sea crew member	Returning resident
Educational exchange (professor or teacher)	
Employee of designated international organisation or NATO	
Fiancé(e) or spouse of US citizen awaiting immigrant visa	
Foreign military personnel stationed in the US	
Intracompany transfer	
Media/journalist	
Student	
Temporary worker in shortage area (e.g. agricultural work)	
Tourist	
Transit	
Victim of trafficking	
Visitor for medical treatment	

Figure 3.2 Summary of US visa categories. **Source:** US Department of State Bureau of Consular Affairs (2019).

bring their families to Singapore and cannot marry a Singaporean. 'Foreign talent' consists of professionals working in sectors such as finance, real estate and education. Such migrants can bring their families to Singapore, can marry a Singaporean and are eligible to apply for permanent residency (Singapore Government Ministry of Manpower, 2019). Different systems of governance mean that border controls operate differently for different groups of people. This will be discussed in more detail in Chapter 7.

Visa applications may be rejected. This may be on the basis of insufficient supporting evidence, or failure to meet the requirements of the particular visa. Applications may also be rejected because the applicant is seen as a potential threat to national security; they may have previous criminal convictions, or links to potentially dangerous organisations. Applications by individuals from certain countries may be viewed with particular suspicion, requiring more detailed application processes. Visas may also be refused if the authorities consider that the applicant may be making a false application, for example, applying for study or tourism when they intend to work and perhaps stay indefinitely. In studying migration and border controls, therefore, it is important to recognise the diversity of migrant flows and how particular groups of migrants may be regarded as 'desirable' or 'undesirable' migrants. Immigration officials, too, through their individual decisions, exert control over their country's borders.

Despite border controls people do enter countries without permission. The terminology used to describe this group of people is controversial. Governments and the media often use the term 'illegal immigrant', but academics and human rights campaigners prefer the term 'undocumented' or 'irregular' immigrant. This acknowledges that while such immigration may not be legal, to use the term 'illegal' in relation to a person or group of people could imply that their entire existence is illegal. The IOM uses the term 'irregular migration' to refer to 'movement that takes place outside the regulatory norms of the sending, transit and receiving countries', (IOM, 2017, p. 299). Campaign groups have increasingly used the slogan 'No one is illegal' or 'No human being is illegal' to stress the humanity of all migrants.

In the case of individuals being found to have entered the country without official permission, having overstayed their visa, or having broken the conditions of entry, states implement deportation processes. In some countries such individuals are kept in detention centres while awaiting trial and deportation.

Government approaches to undocumented migrants can change as their policies change. For example, in the USA the 1986 Immigration Control and Reform Act (ICRA) provided an amnesty for all undocumented migrants without criminal convictions who had arrived before 1982. This meant that they could legally stay in the USA if they had their paperwork approved. The ICRA also introduced stricter controls on immigration for potential new arrivals. More recently, attempts have been made to address the situation of migrants who arrived in the USA without documentation before the age of 18. The Development, Relief and Education for Alien Minors (DREAM) Act has been debated in the US Congress on a number of occasions since it was first proposed in 2001, but it has yet to pass into law. In 2012 President Obama introduced the Deferred Action for Childhood Arrivals (DACA) programme to prevent the deportation of undocumented people who arrived in the USA as children. This programme was ended by President Trump in 2017 as part of his plan to strengthen the country's borders.

Refugees

The power of sovereign states to set migration regulations and processes holds for all forms of migration. However, there are international treaties that shape the regulations for the treatment of individuals fleeing persecution and conflict. Signatories of these treaties are required to have national laws and policies that follow the treaty principles.

During and after both the First and Second World Wars, millions of people were forced to flee from their homes, often across international borders. The need to adopt a common approach to protecting all these displaced people led to the 1951 the UN High Commissioner for Refugees (UNHCR) Convention relating to the Status of Refugees, focusing largely on the European context, and the later 1967 Protocol relating to the Status of Refugees, which expanded the remit to a global scale (UNHCR, 2011). As of August 2019 there were 145 signatories to the Convention (UNHCR, 2019).

Under the 1951 Convention a refugee is a person who:

> ... *owing to well-founded fear of being persecuted for reasons of race, religion, nationality, membership of a particular social group or political opinion, is outside the country of his nationality and is unable or, owing to such fear, is unwilling to avail himself of the protection of that country; or who, not having a nationality and being outside the country of his former habitual residence as a result of such events, is unable or, owing to such fear, is unwilling to return to it.*[1] (UNHCR, 1951, p. 14)

---

[1] Although the Convention, as was common at the time, talks about 'he' and 'his', the definition applies to all people, regardless of gender.

Figure 3.3 Syrian refugee families from Kobanî district in a refugee camp at Suruç, Đanlıurfa, Turkey. Since 2011 many Syrians have fled the civil war, heading into neighbouring Turkey (and beyond). **Photo:** © Orlok/Shutterstock.

Key elements of the definition include the crossing of international borders, the fear of persecution, and that this persecution is on the basis of specified characteristics. In circumstances where individuals fit this definition, they have the right to protection in the host country and cannot be sent back to their country of origin.

The rights of refugees, while clearly laid out in a Convention ratified by nearly all UN member states, are not dealt with in the same way in all countries. This is because sovereign states interpret refugee laws and policies in very different contexts. This acknowledgement of spatial differences and the importance of considering scale is vital to how geographers approach these issues (Willis, 2018). As Laliberté argues in relation to human rights more generally, 'At its most basic, a geographic approach to studying human rights provides the means to examine local variations in the implementation of, and access to "universal" human rights' (2015, p. 58). Each country will have different requirements in terms of the evidence needed to demonstrate 'a well-founded fear of persecution'. Legal processes and legal support will vary, as will the interpretation of evidence (Gill, 2016). In countries with better developed governance systems refugees will be expected to make formal asylum claims on their arrival; elsewhere the sheer number of refugees and resource limitations may mean that formal claims for asylum are not feasible.

Internally displaced persons

People who are forced to leave their homes because of civil unrest or persecution may flee to another part of their own country. These people are classified as internally displaced persons (IDPs). The 1998 UN Guiding Principles on Internal Displacement (UNOCHA, 2001) define internally displaced persons as:

> ... persons or groups of persons who have been forced or obliged to flee or to leave their homes or places of habitual residence, in particular as a result of or in order to avoid the effects of armed conflict, situations of generalized violence, violations of human rights or natural or human-made disasters, and who have not crossed an internationally recognized state border (cited in IOM, 2017, p. 299).

Unlike the international definition of a 'refugee', an IDP can be fleeing a disaster, whether that be natural, such as a flood or earthquake, or human-made, such as a major industrial pollution incident.

Because these flows take place within national territory, international agreements stress that national governments have the primary responsibility for dealing with IDPs and protecting their rights to security, shelter, food and other items covered under the Universal Declaration of Human Rights (UN, 1948).

Figure 3.4 Tents at a Salesian IDP camp, Juba, South Sudan, February 2017. Since 2013 conflict in South Sudan has forced nearly two million people to move within the country. Over three million more have fled to other countries. **Photo:** © Adriana Mahdalova/Shutterstock.

They may need help. Principle 25, point 2 of the UN 'Guiding Principles on Internal Displacement' states:

International humanitarian organizations and other appropriate actors have the right to offer their services in support of the internally displaced. Such an offer should not be regarded as an unfriendly act or an interference in a state's internal affairs and shall be considered in good faith (UNOCHA, 2001, p. 13).

This means that IDP camps may be set up and run by international agencies, such as the International Committee of the Red Cross or UNHCR, if permission is given by the national government.

People trafficking

Many migrants have little choice but to move: they are driven out by war, criminality, poverty or an environmental disaster. These so-called 'push factors' will be discussed further in Chapter 4. A particular group that is denied choice are victims of trafficking, either internally or across international borders.

According to the 2000 UN Protocol to Prevent, Suppress and Punish Trafficking in Persons, Especially Women and Children (UN Office of the High Commissioner on Human Rights (OHCHR), 2000), people trafficking has three elements (Figure 3.5). All three elements must be present for the movement of a person to be defined as 'trafficking'. The three elements involve the act of trafficking, how it is done and for what purpose.

It is important to note that people trafficking is not the same as people smuggling. Smuggling involves the transport of people (the act), and there may be deception about the conditions and costs of the process (the means), but the purpose is not for further exploitation of the migrants.

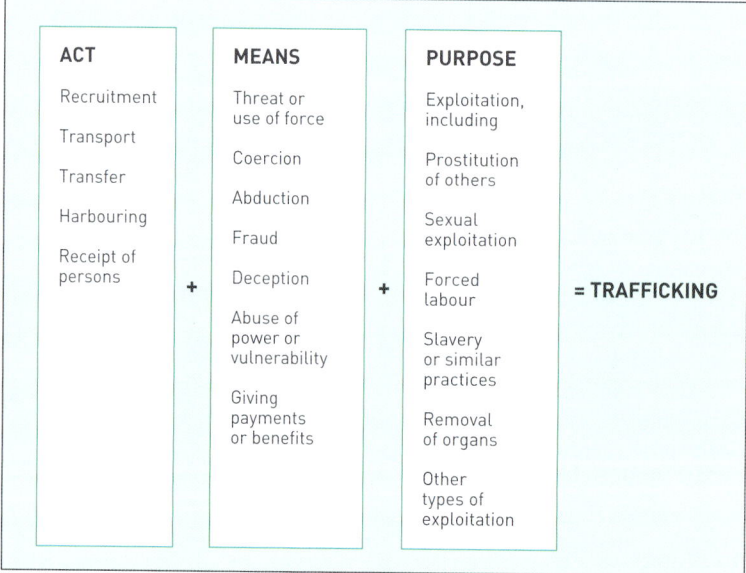

Figure 3.5 The three elements of human trafficking. **Source:** UN Office on Drugs and Crime (UNODC) (2019).

Signatories of the Protocol must ensure that their national laws reflect its spirit, both in preventing trafficking in the first place and then supporting its victims (UNODC, 2019).

Regional co-operation

In a globalising world, regional associations of a number of states have become increasingly common as a way of facilitating trade, expanding markets and promoting stability and security. In many cases, such organisations are trading blocs, with free trade between member states and common trade policies towards non-members; for instance ASEAN or EFTA (European Free Trade Association). The removal of borders between member states for trade purposes is very rarely matched by freedom of movement for people. The European Union (EU), with its freedom of movement policy, is the main exception to this trend. This has greatly facilitated migration for work and study, as well as business travel and tourism. However, in some contexts, freedom of movement throughout the EU has created tensions around access to employment and services, as well as issues of national identity (see Chapters 5 and 6).

As a regional entity with internal freedom of movement, the EU has developed a common set of immigration procedures. Frontex, the European Border and Coastguard Agency, does not have the capacity to police territorial and maritime borders, but it co-ordinates co-operation between the border agencies of member states. Since 2015 there has been a particular focus on addressing the movement of migrants across the Mediterranean. This work has largely focused on preventing migrants reaching European waters, rather than rescuing and supporting refugees (Frontex, 2019).

The 'no borders' movement

The governance of migration in the 21st century is based on a system whereby decisions about immigration are made by national governments within an international system that respects state sovereignty. For some academic researchers and campaigners, restricting human mobility by policing borders creates human rights violations (King, 2016). For example, Jones (2016) argues that it is the very presence of borders, as well as the way they are policed, which leads to increased vulnerability, injury and even death for thousands of people seeking security and a better life. However, the dismantling of border controls would challenge the very basis of the post-Second World War international governance system. It also raises questions about the impact of free movement, and which places and groups of people would be most affected.

Figure 3.6 Syrian refugees arriving on the Greek island of Lesvos, October 2015. **Photo:** © Nicolas Economou/Shutterstock.

Figure 3.7 Protester campaigning against refugee boats being turned back during World Refugee Day rally, Brisbane, Australia, 2015. Australia has a policy of forcing boats carrying asylum seekers to turn back from Australian waters, to prevent them landing on Australian territory.. **Photo:** © paintings/Shutterstock.

ACTIVITY BOX 3

1a Choose a country and find out what visas it makes available. A good place to start would be the website of the embassy or high commission of that country.
1b Classify the visas into groups and explain your categorisation.
1c Which of the visas (if any) reflect the country's obligations under international conventions?
2a Create a Venn diagram using the information in this chapter. In the left-hand circle, put reasons countries may wish to restrict migration. In the right-hand circle, put arguments why countries should not restrict migration. Where the circles overlap list the obligations that countries have signed up to that govern migration.
2b Use colour to categorise the reasons in the diagram: economic, political, human rights, resulting from other treaties and alliances, historical.
2c What patterns emerge from your diagram?
2d To what extent do these reasons help explain the current patchwork of rules governing migration?

References

Frontex (2019). Frontex home page. Available at https://frontex.europa.eu (last accessed 2/9/2019).

Gill, N. (2016) *Nothing Personal? Geographies of governing and activism in the British asylum system.* Chichester: Wiley-Blackwell.

Ho, E.L.-E. (2006) 'Negotiating belonging and perceptions of citizenship in a transnational world: Singapore, a cosmopolis?', *Social & Cultural Geography*, 7, 3, pp. 385–401.

IOM (2017) *World Migration Report 2018*. Available at https://tinyurl.com/y9bz22z5 (last accessed 18/9/2019).

Jones, R. (2016) *Violent Borders: Refugees and the right to move.* London: Verso.

King, N. (2016) *No Borders: the politics of immigration control and resistance.* London: Zed Books.

Laliberté, N. (2015) 'Geographies of human rights: mapping responsibility', *Geography Compass*, 9, 1, pp. 57–67.

OHCHR (2000) *UN Protocol to Prevent, Suppress and Punish Trafficking in Persons, Especially Women and Children.* Available at https://tinyurl.com/y4utsrc3 (last accessed 5/10/2019).

Singapore Government Ministry of Manpower (2019) *Work Passes and Permits.* Available at https://tinyurl.com/hv5t4vm (last accessed 28/8/2019).

Storey, D. (2017) 'States, territory and sovereignty', *Geography*, 102, 2, pp. 116–21.

UN (1945) *Charter of the United Nations.* Available at https://tinyurl.com/pm9zewh (last accessed 10/8/2019).

UN (1948) *Universal Declaration of Human Rights.* Available at https://tinyurl.com/zckj6df (last accessed 5/10/2019).

UNHCR (2011) *The 1951 Convention relating to the Status of Refugees and its 1967 Protocol.* Available at https://tinyurl.com/yxe4w8jo (last accessed 10/8/2019).

UNHCR (2019) *The 1951 Refugee Convention.* Available at https://tinyurl.com/ybqnp6f5 (last accessed 10/8/2019).

UNOCHA (2001) *Guiding Principles on Internal Displacement.* Available at www.unhcr.org/43ce1cff2.html (last accessed 18/9/2019).

UNODC (2019) Human trafficking. Available at https:/tinyurlcom/3p7s5ht (last accessed 2/9/2019).

US Department of State Bureau of Consular Affairs (2019) *Directory of Visa Categories.* Available at https://tinyurl.com/ybf6936p (last accessed 27/8/2019).

Williams, G., Meth, P. and Willis, K. (2014) *Geographies of Developing Areas: The Global South* (2nd edition). London: Routledge.

Willis, K. (2018) 'Gender, development and human rights: exploring global governance', *Geography*, 103, 2, pp. 70–77.

 Extra resources to accompany this chapter are available on the Top Spec web pages. See page 4 for further information.

4. The human experience of migration

The definitions of migration set out in Chapter 3 are essential to measure migration and to establish patterns over time and space. However, we should be careful to recognise their limitations in capturing the complex human experience of migration. Humans do not think about the spaces in which they live their lives in the ordered way suggested by maps. People's lives interact within and between cities, regions and states. Family and friendship groups can be spread across such spaces and therefore identities can span, and be more complex than, easily definable political units. Furthermore, migrants rarely consider the impact of supranational and global governance structures on their lives and choices. Their motivations can include work, security, family reasons and study, and they may blur the distinctions between them. As shown in Chapter 3, these motivations can change over time, as can the international and domestic policies and agreements that currently structure the governance of migration.

Models of migration

Traditionally, geographers have used Lee's (1966) model of push and pull factors, taking into account intervening obstacles, to try to explain migration choices (see Figure 4.2). This model, that can be applied to migrant workers, IDPs and refugees alike, recognises that patterns of migration respond to environmental, economic and political change in both the source and host areas of a migration flow. It suggests that the decision to migrate is based on a balance of positive and negative push and pull factors. If the balance is sufficiently positive to justify the cost of overcoming any intervening obstacles, individuals may decide to migrate.

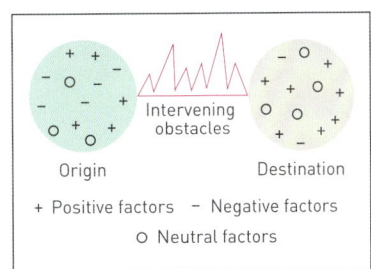

Figure 4.2 The Lee 'push-pull' model of migration. **Source:** Warn et al. (2008), after Lee (1966).

However, different geographers have prioritised different push or pull factors when explaining migration, and altered their models to take account of the influence of the information that migrants may or may not have when making migration choices. This has led to five contrasting models of migration.

Neoclassical economic theory

This states that the most significant push/pull factors are wage differences, so migration tends to flow from low-wage areas to high-wage areas. The model in Figure 4.2 prioritises economic incentives and assumes that migrants have meaningful information about wage differentials. In this model, would-be migrants are economic actors, willing and able to act on what they believe to be in their best interests. It assumes that if there is sufficient economic rationale host countries will not block migration. It further assumes that economic motivation is sufficient to overcome the risks of migration or the personal and cultural costs of moving.

Dual labour market theory

In this model, migration is mainly caused by pull factors in more developed countries. Migrant workers are needed to fill the lowest-paid jobs either because there is a labour shortage or the local population does not wish to do this work. This model also assumes that the most important factors behind migration choices are economic. However it differs from neoclassical economic theory in assuming that actors in the host country actively seek out and enable migration to meet their needs. It regards the host country's desire for migration to be a prerequisite, without which would-be migrants would not have the ability to migrate, regardless of their own economic interests.

Figure 4.1 Young men who have migrated from Afghanistan and Pakistan to Istanbul, Turkey, waiting for the possibility of daily work. **Photo:** © Orlok/Shutterstock.

Post-colonial migration from former colonies to European countries during the post-Second World War economic boom would be a good example.

The new economics of labour migration
This states that migration flows and patterns cannot be explained solely at the level of individual workers and the push and pull factors that incentivise migration. For example, an impoverished household or wider social group can improve its condition through remittances sent back by family members engaged in migrant labour abroad. This model develops neoclassical economic theory by recognising that would-be migrants do not have perfect information about wage differentials, and that their decision to migrate is made in the context of their home community. Migrants move in order to improve the lives of those they leave behind, and they can only overcome the barriers to migration because their family or community provide them with the resources to do so.

Relative deprivation theory
This proposes the spreading awareness in the source community of the new-found affluence of their former neighbours as an important factor in migration. Successful migrants may use their remittances to provide better schooling for their children and a better quality of life for their families, and their former neighbours may wish to emulate their success This helps explain why migrants from the same source region often migrate to the same host region. The importance of the source community and 'word of mouth' information is often replicated in the host country, with enclaves of migrants locating in the same places and working in the same sectors. However, this information may be misleading, or distorted to suit different agendas. For instance, criminal gangs are known to deceive 'information-poor' potential migrants in the source region.

Figure 4.3 Chinese migrant construction workers going home, Huaibei, China.
Photo: © zhaoliang70/Shutterstock.

World systems theory
This looks at migration from a global perspective. Trade between countries with unequal levels of development may create incentives to migrate to the country with a more vibrant economy. For example, Jamaica has a current population of 2 million, but an expatriate community 800,000 strong in its former colonial power, the UK (Wikipedia, 2019). Some geographers argue that even after decolonisation, the economic dependence of former colonies on former colonial powers remains, encouraging migration along traditional routes. Others disagree, arguing that free trade can reduce migration by relocating production from high- to low-wage economies, notwithstanding that the relocation of production is often more controversial than the relocation of labour.

What is the scale of migration?
Globalisation has caused very significant changes in the global economic system, creating the push and pull factors required to drive migration. The two main trends are rural to urban migration, within low and middle HDI countries, and international migration from increasingly connected middle and high HDI countries. Regional and local crises create smaller movements of IDPs and refugees.

Most migration occurs within countries and is a fairly common human experience. In 2009 the United Nations Development Programme estimated that 740 million people – roughly 1 in 10 human beings – had migrated within their country of birth (United Nations Department of Economic and Social Affairs (UN DESA), 2017). Most of these movements will be people taking advantage of opportunities to better their lives as their country's economy develops: in particular, by moving from low productivity work in rural areas to high productivity work in urban areas. A small minority, however, will be IDPs, whose experience of migration is likely to be forced and in response to hardship. In 2017 the Internal Displacement Monitoring Centre estimated that there were 40.3 million IDPs worldwide (UN DESA, 2017).

International migration is less common. The UN DESA in 2019 estimated the total stock of international migrants at 272 million – roughly one in 30 human beings (IOM, 2019a). Again, the majority of these migrants will be responding to opportunities created by trends and changes in the global economy. The majority will be prosperous and well-established in their new place of residence. Only a small number will be refugees. The UN High Commissioner for Refugees (UNHCR) estimated in 2018 that there were 25.9 million refugees, representing only about 9% of international migration (IOM, 2019a).

While it is clear that there is much less international migration than internal migration, and that refugees and IDPs constitute only a small part of the total, all migrations are increasing in scale over time.

International migration has increased from 153 million in 1990 to 272 million in 2019 (Figure 4.4). This increase of two thirds is large. However, when one takes into account the rising global population over this period, the proportion of global population constituted by international migrants has only increased from 2.9% to 3.5%. Regional conflicts, such as in the Syrian Arab Republic, and large-scale population displacement, such as the Rohingya in Myanmar, have ensured that the number of IDPs and refugees also continues to increase. Better global governance and economic growth is likely to contribute to an increase in international migration, but could also contribute to a decrease in internal displacement and refugee movements (IOM, 2019a).

Spatial patterns in migration

As Figure 4.5 shows, the distribution of international migration by continent is unequal. Europe and Asia had the greatest stock of international migrants in 2019; with about 83 million migrants each, these two continents are host to nearly two thirds of the world's international migrants. However, the largest growth in international migration has been in Asia, where about 34 million people have crossed international borders since 2000. This increase is greater than the 2019 total stock of international migrants in each of the three regions with the least migrants: Africa (27 million), Latin America (12 million) and Oceania (9 million). The other region with a large stock of international migrants is North America (the USA and Canada), with 59 million migrants in 2019. The fastest rates of growth in migrant numbers in the period 2000–2019 were in Latin America and Africa, with Asia ranked third (IOM, 2019a). There is also significant variation in host and source countries for international migrants. The USA is the main host country, with 51 million migrants. Within Europe the largest host countries are Germany (13 million), the UK (10 million), France (8 million), Spain (6 million) and Italy (6 million).

INFORMATION BOX 4.1 MIGRANT STOCKS AND MIGRANT FLOWS

International migrant stocks are estimates of 'the total number of international migrants present in a given country at a particular point in time'. UN data on these stocks are based mostly on the number of people in a country's population who were born abroad, and (where this information is not available) who hold foreign citizenship. Data on migrant stocks are often reported together with data on migrant flows. Although both terms account for the number of migrants, what they measure is different. Migrant flows data account for the number of migrants entering or leaving during a specified time period (usually one calendar year) (UN DESA, 2017).

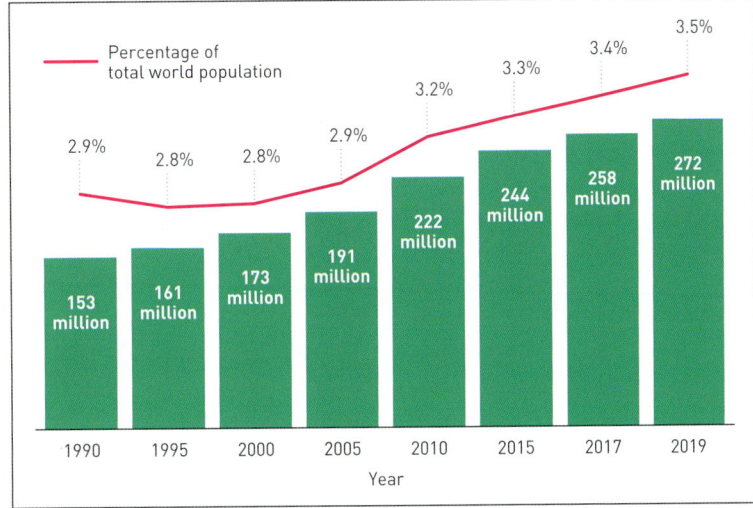

Figure 4.4 Estimates of international migrant population, 1990–2019. **Sources:** IOM (2018, 2019a).

CHAPTER 4

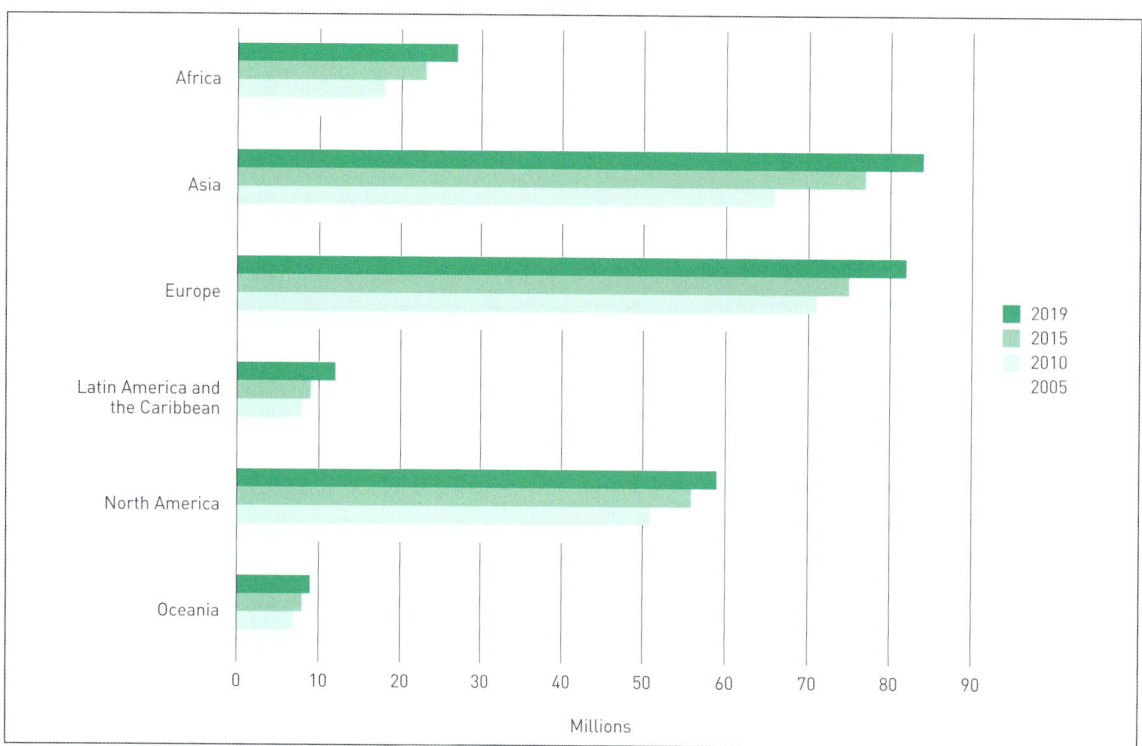

Figure 4.5 International migrants by major region of residence, 2005–2019. **Source:** IOM (2019a, p. 24) using UNDESA (2019) data.

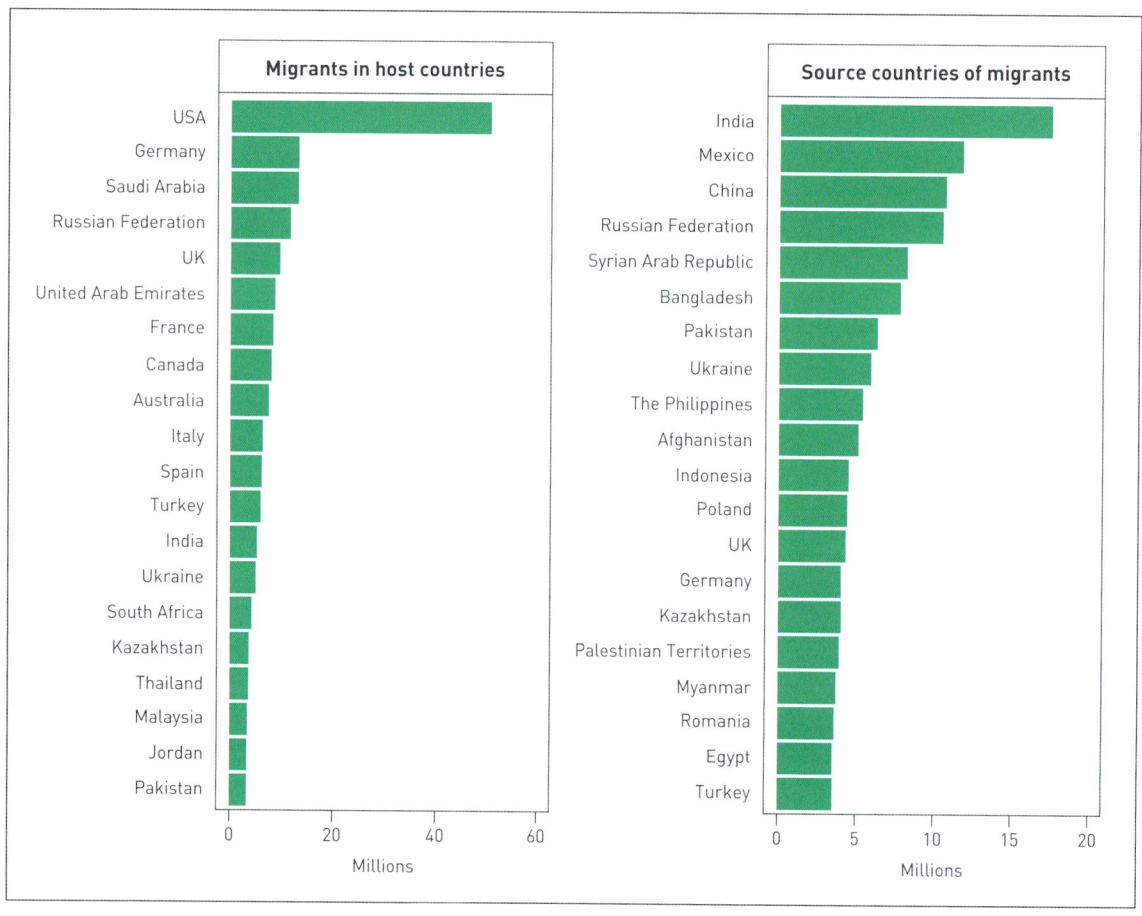

Figure 4.6 Top 20 destinations and origins of international migrants in 2019. **Source:** IOM (2019a, p. 26) using UNDESA (2019) data.

The Russian Federation is a large host country, with 12 million international migrants. Saudi Arabia and United Arab Emirates in the Gulf region are large host nations with 22 million in total (IOM, 2019b).

The largest source of international migrants is India, with 18 million. However, it does not dominate the distribution to the same extent that the USA dominates the list of host nations. Mexico (12 million), the Russian Federation (10.5 million) and China (10.7 million) supply similarly large numbers of emigrants. Many countries have a sizeable stock of emigrants, ranging from 5–8 million; some Asian countries, such as Bangladesh, Pakistan and Afghanistan, belong to this group. Some source countries – for instance Ukraine, the Syrian Arab Repiblic, Turkey and Egypt – neighbour the European Union. The core economy nations of the USA, the UK, Germany and Italy stand out for having a high number of international immigrants and emigrants (although the balance in all cases favours immigration) (IOM, 2019b).

Data on irregular migration is necessarily less reliable, although it is likely to follow a similar pattern. The country with the greatest stock of irregular migrants is the USA, with 11.3 million in 2016. The EU was estimated to host 8 million irregular migrants in 2008, with the UK host to nearly 1 million and Germany host to half a million. The Russian Federation was estimated to host 5–6 million irregular migrant workers in 2011 (IOM, 2017).

This uneven pattern of migration is further reflected in regional migration flows 2000–2015. Asia, at over 30 million, had more than twice Europe's total flow of migrants. Africa and North America had similar total flows of about 10 million, less than a third of Asia's. Latin America was not far behind with 7 million, but Oceania was much lower, with less than 1 million. It is noticeable that the greatest flows in all regions are within each region. For example, 11 million of Asia's emigrants moved to other Asian countries; 5 million of Europe's migrants moved to other European countries. Although most inter-region flows are much smaller, flows from one region to a neighbouring region can be quite large. For example, 4 million migrants moved from Latin America to the USA and nearly 3 million migrants moved from Africa to Europe. Over longer distances, flows between regions tend to be smaller: only 2 million North Americans and slightly fewer Latin Americans moved to Europe. Very small numbers of Europeans moved to Asia and similarly small numbers of Asians moved to Africa. The exception to these small inter-regional flows is out-migrations from Asia. 5 million Asians migrated to Europe and 4 million to North America (IOM, 2017).

Figure 4.7 Migrant fishermen from India in Barbar, Bahrain – an Asia-Asia migration. **Photo:** © John Grummitt/Shutterstock.

CHAPTER 4

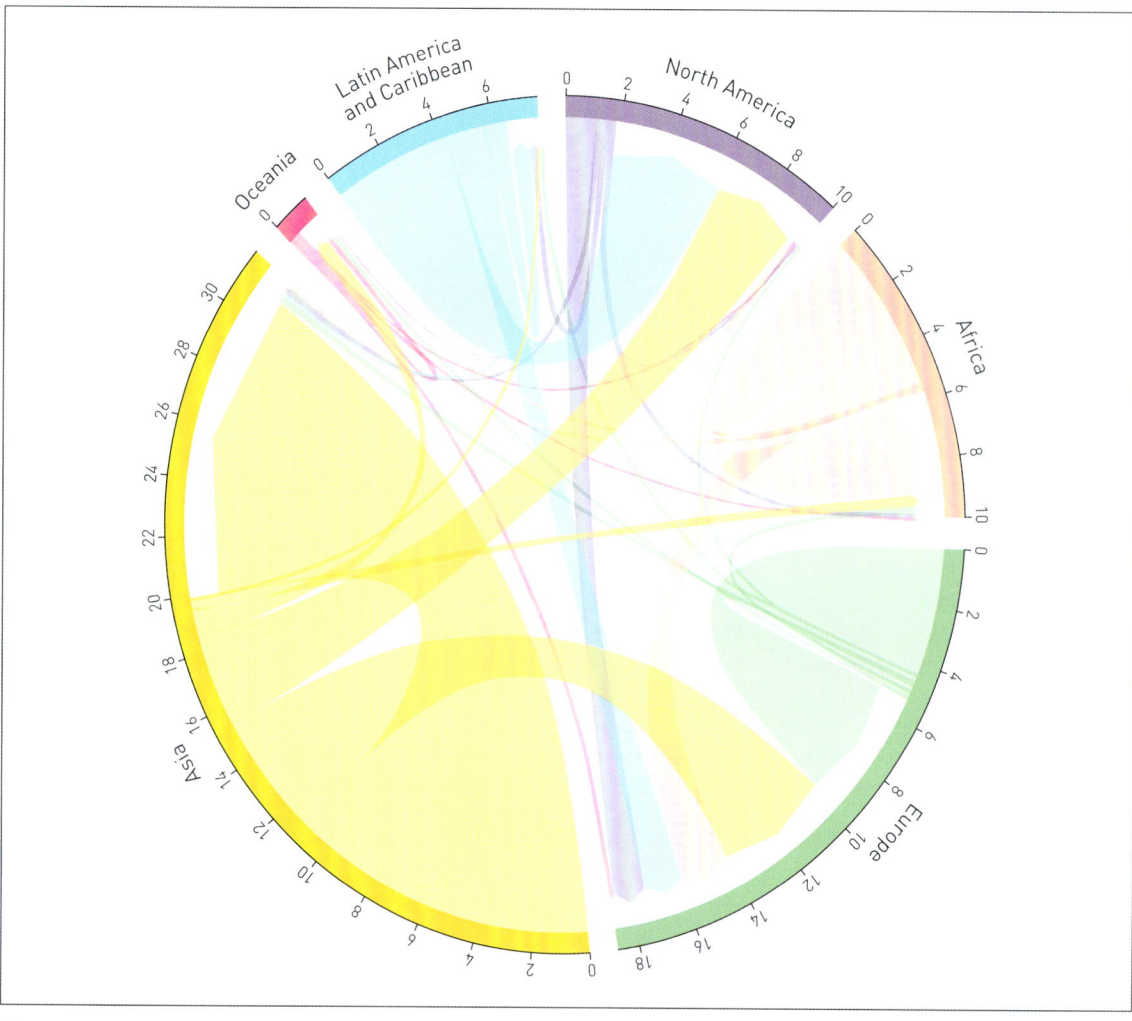

Figure 4.8 Estimated regional migration flows, in millions, 2010–2015. **Source:** IOM (2017).

Types of migrant

Migrant workers

The International Labour Organisation (ILO) estimated the total worldwide stock of migrant workers in 2017 at 164 million. This equates to roughly 70% of all international migrants of working age. 68% of migrant workers go to high-income countries. Construction and domestic service are important sectors for migrant workers, but in high-income countries migrant workers are largely found in service industries such as law, education and business.

Internally displaced persons (IDPs)

The main drivers of internal displacement are conflict, criminal violence and disasters brought on by rapid-onset natural hazards. People can also be displaced by development projects (a new hydroelectric dam, for instance) and slow-onset crises related to drought and environmental change. By 2019 the Internal Displacement Monitoring Centre (IDMC) identified large stocks of IDPs in 56 countries and territories, but over 30 million of the global total of 41.3 million IDPs are located in just 10 countries: The Syrian Arab Republic (6.1 million) and Colombia (5.8 million) are well above the others and together comprise over a quarter of global stocks. They are followed by the Democratic Republic of the Congo (3.1 million), Somalia (2.6 million) and Afghanistan (2.6 million) (IOM, 2019a).

Refugees

UNHCR estimated the total number of refugees worldwide in 2018 to be 25.9 million. A further 3.5 million asylum seekers were awaiting determination of their refugee status. The top 10 countries of origin were the Syrian Arab Republic, Afghanistan, South Sudan, Somalia, Sudan, the DRC, Central African Republic, Myanmar, Eritrea and Burundi. The vast majority of refugees are hosted in neighbouring countries, so the top 10 host nations border the main countries of origin. Turkey is the largest host country in the world, with 3.7 million refugees, mainly Syrians (3.6 million). Jordan and Lebanon are also in the top 10 host nations, for the same reason. Pakistan and the Islamic Republic

MIGRATION AND GLOBAL GOVERNANCE

Figure 4.9 Dereck J Hogan, US Ambassador to Moldova, talks to local government officials at the America Day Fair, Taraclia, Moldova, 2019. **Photo:** ©Piotr Velixar/Shutterstock.

of Iran are also in the top 10 because they take refugees from their neighbour Afghanistan, the second largest origin country. It is often the least developed countries that host the largest numbers of refugees: in 2018 Bangladesh, Chad, the DRC, Ethiopia, Rwanda, South Sudan, Sudan, Tanzania, Uganda and Yemen hosted 33% of the world's refugees (IOM, 2019a).

Elite migration

As defined by the UK Border Agency, elite migrants must be 'internationally recognised as world leaders or potential world-leading talent'. This might include entrepreneurs who want to set up or take over a business. It could include those who want to make a substantial financial investment, a provision aimed at high-net-worth individuals (HNWIs) – typically, people with a minimum of £1 million (US$1.28 million) to invest. It also includes multinational intracompany transfers of employees to manage FDIs. The definition also takes in celebrities, sportspeople and those earning the highest salaries (UK Border Agency, 2019).

Elite migration is disproportionately concentrated in OECD countries, which host two thirds of high-skilled migrants despite comprising only a fifth of global population. The USA, the UK, Canada and Australia host nearly 70% of all skilled migrants. The USA alone hosts nearly half of all elite migrants to OECD countries and one third of high-skilled migrants worldwide. Within countries, elite migration is concentrated in global cities, such as New York, Mexico City and Manila (Goldin *et al*, 2018).

Regional migration corridors

Asia-to-Asia is the largest regional migration corridor in the world. 63 million migrants born in an Asian country now reside in a different Asian country. It is also a very active corridor. Between 2010 and 2017 Asia-to-Asia migration increased by 1.7 million every year. Within this corridor there are large flows from the Indian subcontinent to the Gulf region.

Europe-to-Europe is the second largest regional migration corridor. 41 million migrants born in a European country now reside in a different European country. The rate of migration is smaller than Asia-to-Asia. Since 2000 the annual increase in the number of Europe-to-Europe migrants has been around 0.6 million every year, Romania to Italy and Spain being a large bilateral flow.

The corridor from Latin America and the Caribbean to the USA was the third largest in 2017, with 26 million migrants. The amount of migration via this corridor is in decline, from an average of 0.9 million between 1990 and 2000 to only 0.3 million between 2010 and 2017. Migration from Mexico to the USA is the largest flow, but the pattern is similar for all countries in the region.

Asia-to-Europe is the fourth largest corridor: 20 million Asian migrants reside in Europe. The amount of migration via this corridor is also declining.

The fifth largest corridor is Africa-to-Africa, with 19 million international migrants in 2017. Between 2010 and 2017, the amount of Africa-to-Africa migration increased faster than all other corridors, except for Asia-to-Asia. South Sudan to Uganda is a significant example (UN DESA, 2017).

INFORMATION BOX 4.2
THE BRANDT LINE

In 1980, in a report for the Independent Commission on International Development Issues (ICIDI, 1980), Willy Brandt, the then Chancellor of West Germany, argued that a great chasm in the standard of living existed along a North-South divide. This divide, between the Global North and Global South, is shown in Figure 4.11.

Figure 4.10 Migrant workers from Myanmar harvesting cabbages at Ban Chibabo, Tak, Thailand – another example of Asia-Asia migration. **Photo:** © Somrerk Witthayanant/Shutterstock.

The Brandt Report argued that countries north of the divide are extremely wealthy due to their successful trade in manufactured goods, whereas countries south of the divide are poor because their exports consist of raw materials or intermediate goods that generate low incomes. This division of the world is now challenged by geographers as many countries south of the divide have opened up their economies to globalisation since 1980 and experienced economic benefits as a result. However, the concept remains helpful when exploring changes in patterns of migration.

South-south migration

As we have seen, elite migration historically has been greatest between core economies in the Global North. This has been called north-north migration. Flows of temporary workers has also been greatest from the south to the north. This has been called south-north migration. Of the 64 million international migrants added in the north between 1990 and 2017, 76% were born in the south. However, since 1990 there has been a boom in south-south migration. Between 1990 and 2017, the migrant population originating in and living in the south grew by 70% from 57 million to 97 million. Of the 41 million foreign-born persons added in the south during this period, 96% were born elsewhere in the south, whereas just 4% originated in a

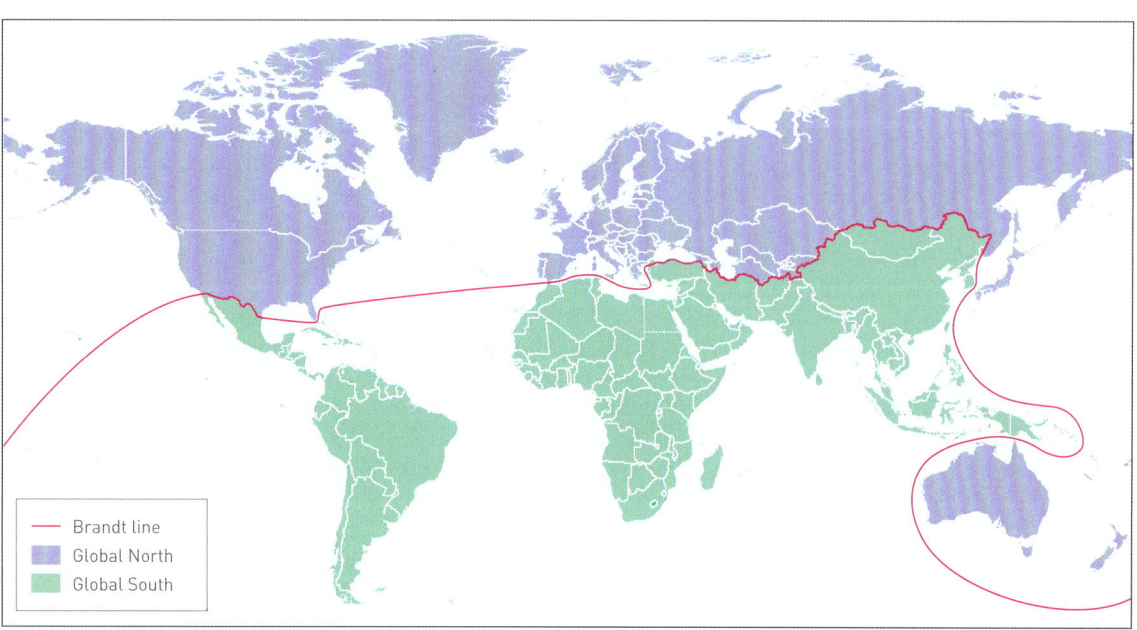

Figure 4.11 The Brandt line. **Source:** Wikimedia Commons (2015) licensed CC BY-SA 4.0.

country of the north. This is strong evidence that economic incentives explain patterns of migration, but that levels of migration only become significant when countries begin to attain a higher level of economic growth and interdependence within regional and global networks (UN DESA, 2017).

Rural to urban migration in semi-periphery economies

According to the ILO, since 1979 China has experienced the largest internal migration ever recorded. China has a total of 229.8 million migrant workers, of whom around 70% are employed in eastern China. Two thirds of these work in large or medium-sized cities, and two thirds of these in manufacturing and construction industries.

These workers are known as the 'floating population'. Chinese citizens are registered in their place of birth by the *hukou* system. Rural citizens do not have an urban *hukou* and cannot easily regularise their relocation to the city; as a result, they are often denied access to housing, health care and education. Despite this official obstacle the pressures to migrate, exacerbated by globalisation, are so strong that it has been estimated that by 2025 a further 250 million Chinese people will migrate from their rural homes to the cities, taking the Chinese urban population over 1 billion (ILO, 2018).

Rural to urban migration in periphery economies

The Democratic Republic of the Congo (DRC) is Africa's second largest nation by land area, with a population of close to 70 million that is growing by nearly 3% annually. The UNDP ranks the DRC's HDI 176th out of 188 countries (UNDP, 2019). The DRC has seen significant rural to urban migration in the last two decades. The population of the capital Kinshasa has doubled in size every five years since 1950 and now has an estimated population of between 11 and 14 million.

INFORMATION BOX 4.3 RURAL TO URBAN MIGRATION

The urban population of the world has grown rapidly, from 751 million in 1950 to 4.2 billion in 2018. This is projected to increase to 7.7 billion by 2050. Together, India, China and Nigeria will account for 35% of the projected growth of the world's urban population between 2018 and 2050. By 2050, it is projected that India will have added 416 million urban dwellers, China 255 million and Nigeria 189 million (UN DESA, 2018). Migration from rural areas within these countries is estimated to be responsible for up to half of this growth; the remainder is due to natural population growth (Tacoli *et al.*, 2015). However, rural to urban migration in higher HDI countries has different characteristics from low HDI countries in sub-Saharan Africa. Migration only accounts for about one third of urban population growth in sub-Saharan Africa, the world region with by far the highest urban population growth rate (4% a year). The contribution of migration is considerably higher in Asia, where urban dwellers constitute almost 60% of the population, a percentage that is expected to continue growing, although at a declining rate.

Figure 4.12 Migrant workers in Shanghai, China. **Photo:** © Yaorusheng/Shutterstock.

Rural to urban migration here is driven almost exclusively by push factors. According to the African Development Bank, 72% of rural households are poor, nearly 40% of children under five suffer from chronic malnutrition and most of the population lives under conditions of moderate to serious food insecurity. Migrants fleeing poverty and conflict in their home provinces move to peri-urban areas or cities in search of work. However, due to the dysfunction of the state and economy there is little or no formal employment in the cities. The majority of migrants rely on informal employment such as street hawking. Wages are so low that researchers have coined the phrase 'the wage puzzle' because it is unclear how these populations are able to survive (African Development Bank, 2013).

Figure 4.13 Food market in Kinshasa, Democratic Republic of Congo. **Photo:** © Ernesto Martin/Shutterstock.

ACTIVITY BOX 4

1a 'I am a migrant' (iamamigrant.org/stories) is a campaign run jointly by the International Labour Organisation and the Joint Council for the Welfare of Migrants to enable migrants to tell their migration stories. Read one or more migrant stories on the website.
1b Create a Venn diagram to summarise the push and pull factors recorded in each story. Include the intervening obstacles where the circles overlap.
1c Analyse the factors in the story and make a judgement about which are the most significant factors in explaining the migration.
2 Explain why there is more rural to urban migration than international migration.
3 Making reference to Chapter 2, outline the reasons why south-south migration, the Asia-Asia corridor and the Africa-Africa corridor are seeing the fastest growth in migration.

References

African Development Bank (2013) *Democratic Republic of Congo: 2013–2017 Country Strategy Paper.* Available at https://tinyurl.com/y3sztvss (last accessed 26/8/2019).

Goldin, I., Pitt, A., Nabarro, B. and Boyle, K. (2018) *Migration and the Economy.* Oxford: Citi GPS/Oxford Martin School. Available at https://tinyurl.com/y4emoe52.

ILO (2018) *Global Estimates on International Migrant Workers.* Geneva: ILO.

ICIDI (1980) *North-South: A program for survival.* The Report of the Independent Commission on International Development Issues under the Chairmanship of Willi Brandt. Cambridge, MA: MIT Press.

IOM (2017) *World Migration Report 2018.* Geneva: IOM.

IOM (2019a) *World Migration Report 2020.* Geneva: IOM.

IOM (2019b) *Migration Data Portal.* Available at https://migrationdataportal.org (last accessed 30/11/2019).

Lee, E.S. (1966) 'A theory of migration', *Demography,* 3, 1, pp. 47–57.

Tacoli, C., McGranahan, G. and Satterthwaite, D. (2015) *Urbanisation, Rural–Urban Migration and Urban Poverty.* London: International Institute for Environment and Development.

UK Border Agency (2019) *Work in the UK.* Available at www.gov.uk/browse/visas-immigration/work-visas (last accessed 26/8/2019).

UN DESA (2017) *International Migration Report 2017.* Geneva: UN.

UN DESA (2018) *World Urbanization Prospects 2018* Available at https://population.un.org/wup (last accessed 20/8/2019).

UNDP (2019) *Human Development Reports.* Available at http://hdr.undp.org/en/countries (last accessed 20/8/2019).

Warn, S., Hordern, B., Witherick, M., Dunn, C., Oakes, S. and Holmes, D. (2008) *Edexcel AS Geography.* Deddington: Philip Allan Updates.

Wikipedia (2019) *Jamaican diaspora.* Available at https://tinyurl.com/y44t5czt (last accessed 1/10/2019).

 Extra resources to accompany this chapter are available on the Top Spec web pages. See page 4 for further information.

5. The consequences of migration

Figure 5.1 Apulia, southern Italy: young people move away from rural areas to more economically dynamic urban areas.
Photo: © Angyalosi Beata/Shutterstock.

Introduction

It is impossible to make definitive statements about the consequences of migration because of the different forms that migration takes, the diversity of people and places involved, and because the consequences vary by scale. In this chapter we will consider scale at the national level (of both the host and the source country), and at community, household and individual levels. We will focus on labour or economic migration as this is numerically the most important form of migration, and is at the heart of studies on the impacts of migration. However, we will also consider the impacts of the flows of refugees and IDPs on their hosts, and on the displaced individuals themselves.

The source country/region
'Brain drain' or 'brain gain'?
Since the 1950s perspectives on the relationship between migration and development in source countries or regions have fluctuated between optimism and pessimism (de Haas, 2010). In the post-Second World War period, researchers argued that migration would have a positive effect on source countries due to the flows of money and ideas that migrants would send back. However, in the 1960s and 1970s the phrase 'brain drain' was coined to describe a negative perspective on emigration. This was because it was usually the younger, better educated, more energetic individuals who left, taking their talents and potential to more economically dynamic locations. This created a vicious circle: source countries or regions stagnated, encouraging more outmigration to locations where the migrants contributed to ongoing economic success (Figure 5.2). Brain drain was associated with increasing inequality between countries, or regions within countries. For example, Michael Lipton (1977) argued in his book *Why Poor People Stay Poor* that rural-urban migration was driven by perceived opportunities in the towns and cities. This led to the decline of the rural areas, so driving more outmigration.

In contrast to the pessimistic brain drain approach, some research highlighted the possibility of 'brain gain', or 'brain circulation':

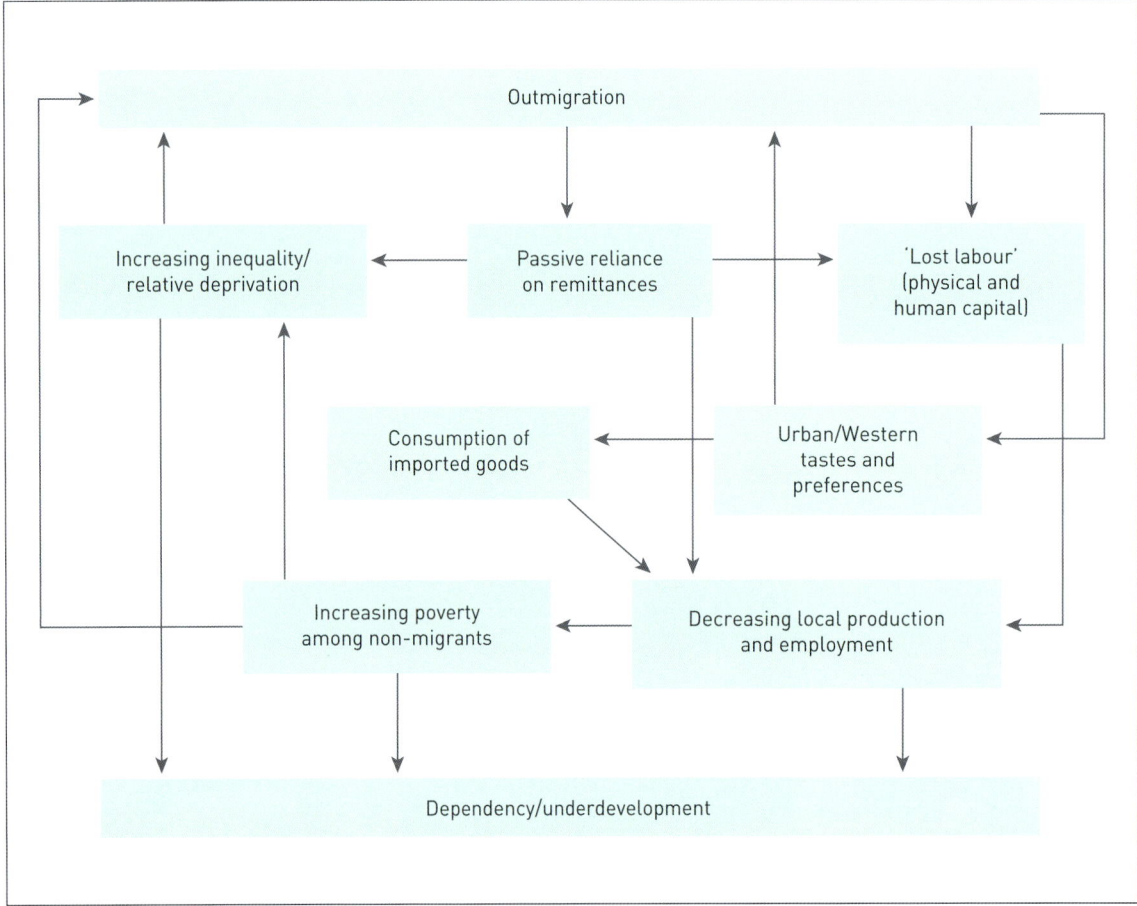

Figure 5.2 Vicious circle of outmigration. **Source:** Adapted from de Haas (2010, p. 237).

the ongoing links between the migrants and their families and home communities would benefit the source country or district. These links could involve flows not only of money, but also of expertise due to the migrants' education, training and experience in the host society. The positive outcomes of migration were, however, sometimes overstated.

Rather than a simple positive or negative interpretation of migration impacts, migration researchers now often stress the importance of the characteristics of the migrants, the nature of the economy and society in the source country, and the context of the host country. For example, in Figure 5.3 outmigration may be a response to social and economic inequality and individuals seeking to improve their lives through access to education and income elsewhere. Conversely, higher levels of education and/or income may make it easier to move away. Remittances sent back to the home community may be spent on goods and services (including education), or be invested in local businesses. This process may create economic growth and job opportunities and reduce household poverty; or it may increase inequality between the households involved in migration and those with no migrants, so encouraging more outmigration.

Remittances

Providing an additional source of income is perceived as one of the main benefits of outmigration for a source country. Globally, remittances are a significant source of foreign currency and are often more stable than private financial flows (see Figure 5.5).

Some countries encourage their citizens to migrate overseas for work, but to retain links with their country of origin. For example, in 1982 the Philippines government set up the Philippine Overseas Employment Administration (POEA). This aims to facilitate the recruitment of Philippine citizens for work overseas and reduce the risk of them being exploited. It licenses foreign recruiters and providing migrant workers with advice and support, though this is not always successful. In 2017 an estimated 2.3 million Filipinos (approximately 1.08 million men and 1.26 million women) were working overseas, mostly in East or Western Asia (Philippine Statistics Authority, 2019). Remittances sent back by these migrants were calculated as US$32.8 billion in 2017, equivalent to just under 10% of the Philippines' GDP (KNOMAD, 2019).

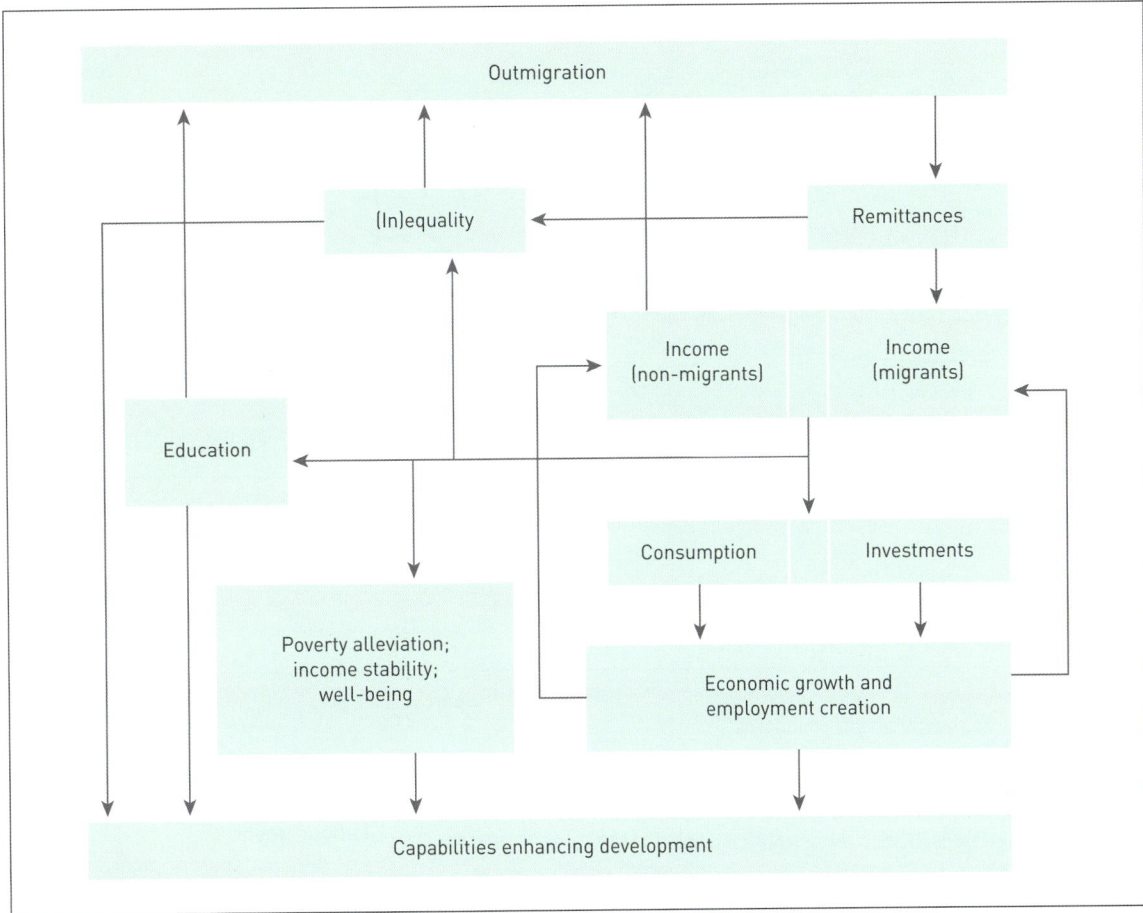

Figure 5.3 The complex relationships between migration and development. **Source:** Adapted from de Haas (2010, p. 251).

Figure 5.4 Money transfer office in Blantyre, Malawi. **Photo:** © Katie Willis.

The impact of remittances on development depends not only on the sums involved, but also on what they are used for. Sometimes remittance recipients are criticised for spending money on electrical items, housing or vehicles, which are not seen as positive investments for economic growth. This criticism fails to recognise the possible multiplier effects of local consumer spending, as well as the benefits that could accrue to an individual, household or community, such as better health due to improved standards of living. Some governments have developed incentive schemes to encourage the investment of remittances in local businesses. Since 2002, Mexico's 3x1 scheme has provided matched funding for remittances from the USA that are invested in local infrastructure projects.

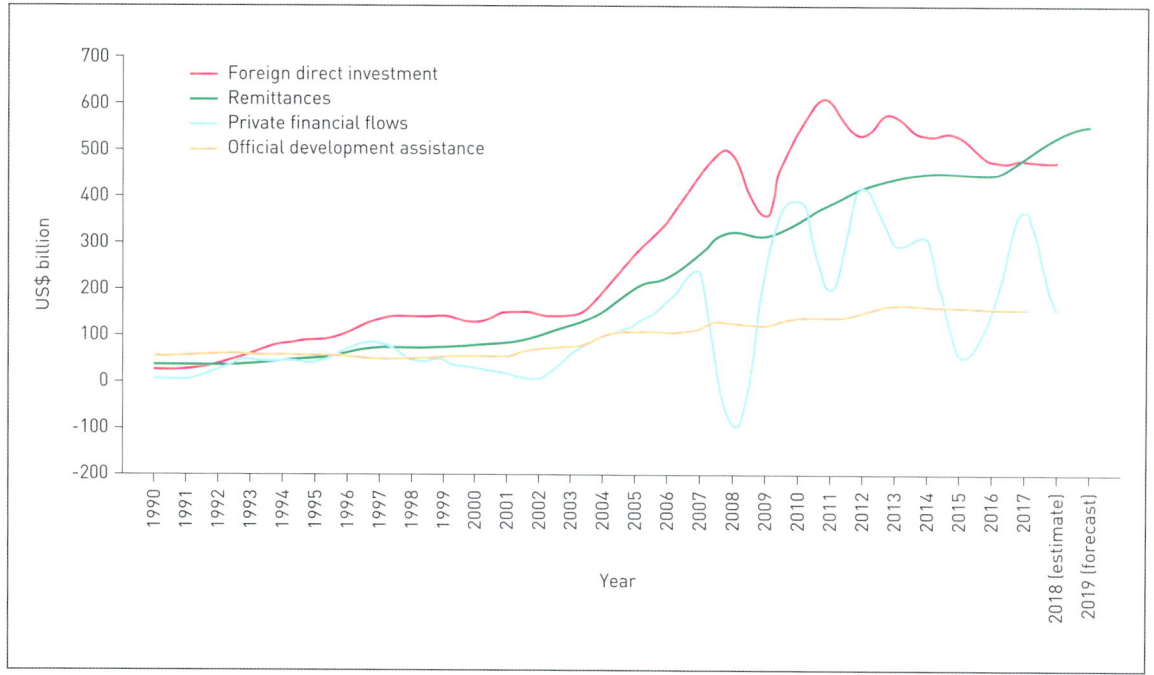

Figure 5.5 Financial flows to low- and middle-income countries, 1990–2019. **Source:** The World Bank, Remittance Inflows. Available at www.knomad.org/data/remittances

INFORMATION BOX 5.1 INTERNATIONAL FINANCIAL FLOWS

Foreign direct investment (FDI): Investment by a government or business in an enterprise in another country.

Official development assistance (ODA): Funds which are given to developing countries, or lent to them at a concessional rate, by governments or international organisations with the main purpose of promoting economic development and welfare.

Private financial flows: Investment in stocks and shares or other financial products by private individuals or organisations.

Remittances: Funds sent back to family members and source communities by migrants.

Financial consequences
Migration reflects both the migrants' need or desire to migrate and their ability to do so. The regions of the Philippines are highly diverse in their levels of economic and human development. In general, the regions in the Luzon island group in the north of the country are wealthier, more urbanised and more economically developed, while those in Mindanao in the south are poorer and more rural, with lower levels of human development as measured by the HDI. The northern provinces have higher rates of labour outmigration, so the remittance benefits are concentrated in those regions that are already better off. Internal migration, particularly to the capital city region of Metro Manila or the export-processing zones, may be more feasible for the populations of marginalised regions; it may also act as a stepping stone to international migration (Clausen, 2010).

The host country
Labour needs
For the host country, migrants can provide a vital labour force which contributes to national economic growth, as well as staffing key public services. The work visa system of many countries is partly based on filling vacancies where there is a perceived shortage of local staff. This may be because such jobs and working conditions – for example agricultural labour, domestic service or construction work – are seen as undesirable by the local work force. Labour shortages may also result from a lack of appropriately skilled and trained staff locally.

Agricultural workers in the USA
In 2016 migrants made up approximately 46.2% of the USA's total agricultural workforce. That figure rose to 56.8% for agricultural labourers (US Department of Agriculture, 2019). Of course these are official figures, so do not include informally employed workers who may be irregular migrants. The reliance of US agriculture on immigrant labour has a long

Figure 5.6 Seasonal immigrant workers harvest and package lettuces in the Salinas Valley, central California. **Photo:** © David Litman/Shutterstock.

Rank	Nationality	Number
1	UK/British	1,021,257
2	Indian	21,207
3	Filipino	18,584
4	Irish	13,320
5	Polish	9272
6	Portuguese	7178
7	Nigerian	6770
8	Italian	6396
9	Spanish	5899
10	Romanian	4451

Figure 5.7 Top ten reported nationalities of NHS staff, March 2019. **Source:** Adapted from Baker (2019), p. 3.

history, but the US government has adopted a range of schemes to balance out labour demand with migration control. The 'Bracero Program[1]', from 1942 to 1964, consisted of a series of agreements between the US and Mexican governments to allow for seasonal migration of agricultural workers from Mexico to the US. During this period 4.6 million individual worker contracts were signed (Bracero History Archive, 2019). The program ended partly because of complaints that it was depressing the wages of American agricultural workers and causing a decline in working conditions. Subsequent US government schemes to permit entry for seasonal agricultural workers have been on a much smaller scale.

Workers in urban areas

In urban areas, immigrants make significant contributions across the economy, from childcare and gardening in private residences, to running small and medium-sized businesses, professional roles in medicine, law and finance, and heading international corporations. In Silicon Valley, California, approximately 71% of the high-tech employees are immigrants (Balk, 2018); they are also very important in creating start-up companies in the region. In Seattle, Washington State, foreign-born IT workers make up 40% of the IT labour force (Balk, 2018). Without these immigrants, key sectors of the US economy would either not be able to function, or be less dynamic. However, there are debates around potential impacts on opportunities for US citizens (see below).

Public service workers

Immigrant workers can also be key for the delivery of public services. In the UK, the post-Second World War establishment of the National Health Service (NHS) and the expansion of public transport needed workers. With insufficient available labour within the UK, targeted recruitment campaigns encouraged the citizens of Commonwealth countries to move to Britain (Younge, 2018). NHS reliance on foreign-born workers continues today: in March 2019 NHS staff in England reported being of 212 nationalities. While British citizens were far and away the largest group, Figure 5.7 shows that other nationalities in the top ten came from countries in Africa, Asia and Europe.

Labour migration is not just a Global South to Global North phenomenon. As outlined in the previous chapter, the Africa–Africa corridor is the fifth largest in the world. While refugees make up about one-third of this movement, migration for employment is also significant. For example, there are important labour migration circuits in southern Africa for mining and large-scale commercial agriculture. Labour migration also occurs from the Global North to the Global South in sectors such as education and development assistance, as well as transnational corporations.

Potential tensions

While migrants make significant contributions to the economies of host countries, there can be tension between local people and migrants, especially when they are perceived as taking jobs from locals and/or depressing local wages: this was the case with the Bracero Program

---

[1] '*bracero*' is an early 20th-century Spanish term for a manual labourer.

in the USA. The reliance on foreign staff in the USA's high-tech industry has also attracted criticism. Sites such as Silicon Valley and Seattle have benefitted greatly from the IT skills and dynamism of immigrant workers. These workers have been able to enter the US because their particular skills make them eligible for H-1B visas, which are designed to recruit employees into sectors where there is a domestic shortage. However, there have been complaints that in some cases immigrant labour has been hired despite there being highly competent American candidates. The efforts of President Trump's administration to clamp down on foreign recruitment has led to conflict with high-technology firms (Baron, 2019).

Another possible cause of tension between migrants and the local population can be the allocation of services. Immigrants need access to housing, education and health services, and there may be a perception on the part of the host population that these newcomers are given priority. As outlined in Chapter 2, part of migration governance is setting out the rights that immigrants have once they have legally entered a country. Some national governments make significant distinctions between the rights of citizens and immigrants, or particular groups of immigrants (the distinction between 'foreign workers' and 'foreign talent' in Singapore, for example).

Refugee camps

In some parts of the world, refugees or IDPs are accommodated in camps, often in tents or other temporary shelter. These settlements may be formally established and managed by a government agency, an NGO or the UNHCR, or they may be unofficial, as in the case of the so-called 'Jungle' camp in Calais, northern France. Life for residents in these camps can be challenging and is often very precarious, particularly in the unofficial camps. The arrival of a large number of refugees in a short period of time can put particular pressures on host governments and societies. For example, 1.3 million Syrians have fled to neighbouring Jordan since the outbreak of civil war in 2011 (Wahba, 2019).

While refugee/IDP camps are often intended to be temporary places of refuge, providing security for vulnerable people while their claims are being processed, or until they return home, some refugee camps have become established settlements and communities. This is because the inhabitants do not feel safe to return home, but they have not been allowed to move elsewhere within the host country. Over time, residents may also have developed businesses and social networks that provide incentives to stay. The Dadaab camp near the Somali border in eastern Kenya was established in 1991 to house refugees fleeing the civil war in Somalia. It now consists of four different camps housing over 210,000 refugees and asylum seekers (UNHCR, 2019). The Dadaab complex is home to thousands of families – generations have grown up there. However, for the Kenyan government the camp represents a drain on scarce resources; it is also seen as a security risk. The militant group al-Shabaab claimed responsibility for deadly attacks in Kenya, including on the Westgate shopping mall in Nairobi in 2013 and Garissa University College in northern Kenya in 2015. The government regards the Dadaab camp as the seedbed that nurtured and radicalised these militants; they want the camp closed (Rawlence, 2016). The Kenyan High Court blocked a planned closure in 2017 as contravening Kenya's international responsibilities, but the government is continuing to call for its closure and is demanding that UNHCR, which runs the camp, supports the residents in returning to their country of origin, or relocating elsewhere outside Kenya.

Cultural impacts

Migrants bring with them their language, dress, cultural norms and daily practices. Moving to another country may result in changes in these practices, but often they are reproduced in the host society. Migrants may choose to live in neighbourhoods where there are other people from the same ethnic group as this gives them a sense of familiarity and security in a new environment. Demographic changes in an area may contribute to changes in its nature, and the way it is experienced and represented.

Figure 5.8 Little India, Singapore. **Photo:** © Katie Willis.

Language, dress and behaviour are often very visible practices. In host societies that do not share the migrants' culture, these visible differences can exacerbate tensions between local populations and migrant communities. Host populations may feel that their identity and way of life is threatened by the arrival of migrant groups they do not see as sharing their values and norms. This is discussed in more detail in Chapter 6.

The consequences for individuals
The migrants

For both individuals and households, migration can provide opportunities to escape poverty and economic vulnerability. Wages that host country nationals regard as too low may provide a significant boost to a migrants' income and family life chances. Migration may also be an opportunity for career advancement. Travelling overseas may provide migrants with access to training or job opportunities not available in their home country.

However, when they move countries, skilled migrants may discover that their qualifications and experience are not recognised in the host country. Medicine, law, social work and finance are among the sectors where professional accreditation may not easily transfer. This is most likely to occur when migrants are moving from the Global South to the Global North. In such cases, migrants who were professionals in their home countries may have to take lower-skilled and lower-paid work in the host country. For example, many Filipina women who have trained as nurses or other healthcare professionals in the Philippines take on jobs as care assistants when they migrate because of the difficulty of transferring their qualifications (IOM, 2012). In some cases, these women hire carers and domestic help in the Philippines to look after the family they have left behind. This process is part of what Arlie Hochschild (2000) termed 'global care chains'.

Figure 5.9 Workers at the Googleplex headquarters, Mountain View, USA.
Photo: © Anton Gvozdikov/Shutterstock.

Many migrants are looking for a better life not just for themselves, but for their families. In particular, they may focus on improving the life chances of their children. In such cases the benefits of migration may not be directly felt by the adult migrant; in fact they may experience significant hardship and loss of professional status. They accept this in the hope that their children will have greater opportunities than themselves, either because the money they send back home will provide a better education or life chances for their children. If the children have come with them, they will have a better education and economic opportunities, which can lead to social mobility. Migration can contribute to inter-generational transfers whereby children inherit money and other resources from their parents.

The people and communities left behind

Migration affects not just the people who move, but the people they leave behind. They may benefit from money and goods sent home from abroad, but in some cases remittances may not be sent, or may reduce or cease over time. This may result in greater impoverishment than before for the family members left behind. They may also experience increased work responsibilities: looking after children, running a family business or tending crops and raising animals. While such responsibilities may be a burden – heavy workloads causing health problems – the need to take on new responsibilities and develop new skills can be a positive. McEvoy et al. (2012) studied the impact of male outmigration on a rural community in the Mexican state of Campeche. With many men absent in the USA, women's agricultural workloads increased, but they also took on additional decision-making responsibilities. Some women viewed this very positively, but others were unsure about the additional burdens; they also worried about the potential for gossip among the neighbours when their new responsibilities brought them into contact with male members of the community.

Peggy Levitt (1998) coined the term 'social remittances' to describe the transfer of ideas that occurs as a result of migration. The benefits from migration may not be confined to material goods or money, but can also include ideas and behaviours drawn from migrants' observations and experiences while overseas. Such social remittances could include business ideas, political opinions and social norms around parenting or gender relations.

Migration can have significant emotional impacts, on both migrants and non-migrants. Family separation can be painful, particularly when parents migrate leaving their children behind. Parents may be doing this to help their children in material terms, but emotionally it comes at a cost (Basa et al., 2011). Technology has greatly helped migrants keep in touch with family members at home, but this is not the same as being physically present.

Refugees

Finally, we must acknowledge that for some migrants the migration journey is very hazardous. The IOM's Missing Migrants Project recorded over 32,000 migrant deaths between 2014 and 2018, but this is likely to be a significant underestimate. During this period more than 17,900 people died or went missing trying to cross the Mediterranean, just over 1900 people died trying to cross the Mexico-US border and nearly 2200 deaths were reported in Southeast Asia, largely of Rohingya fleeing persecution in Myanmar (IOM, 2019, p. viii). Even if refugees arrive safely at their destination, they may then experience marginalisation, racism and discrimination.

References

Baker, C. (2019) *NHS Staff from Overseas: Statistics.* House of Commons Library Briefing Paper, No. 7783, 8 July. Available at https://tinyurl.com/yxbrq37f (last accessed 14/9/2019).

Balk, G. (2018) 'More than half of Seattle's software developers were born outside U.S.', *The Seattle Times*, 17 January. Available at https://tinyurl.com/yxzrnbnv (last accessed 14/9/2019).

Baron, E. (2019) 'H-1B visa: Approvals dropped sharply last year, keep falling this year', *The Mercury News*, 4 June. Available at https://tinyurl.com/y2v7d3a3 (last accessed 14/9/2019).

Basa, C., Harcourt, W. and Zarro, A. (2011) 'Remittances and transnational remittances in Italy and The Philippines: Breaking the global care chain', *Gender and Development*, 19, 1, pp. 11–22.

Bracero History Archive (2019). Available at http://braceroarchive.org/about (last accessed 2/9/2019).

Clausen, A. (2010) 'Economic globalization and regional disparities in the Philippines', *Singapore Journal of Tropical Geography*, 31, 3, pp. 299–316.

de Haas, H. (2010) 'Migration and development: a theoretical perspective', *International Migration Review*, 44, 1, pp. 227–64.

Hochschild, A.R. (2000) 'Global care chains and emotional surplus value' in Hutton, W. and Giddens, A. (eds) *On The Edge: Living with Global Capitalism.* London: Jonathan Cape.

IOM (2012) *Crushed Hopes: Underemployment and deskilling among skilled migrant women.* Available at https://tinyurl.com/y4zlfceh (last accessed 14/9/2019).

IOM (2019) *Fatal Journeys Volume 4.* Available at https://tinyurl.com/y3bseq2h (last accessed 14/9/2019).

KNOMAD (2019) *Remittances data.* Available at www.knomad.org/data/remittances (last accessed 2/9/2019).

Levitt, P. (1998) 'Social remittances: migration driven local-level forms of cultural diffusion', *International Migration Review*, 32, 4, pp. 926–48.

Lipton, M. (1977) *Why Poor People Stay Poor: Urban bias in world development.* Cambridge, MA: Harvard University Press.

McEvoy, J., Petrzelka, P., Radel, C. and Schmook, B. (2012) 'Gendered mobility and morality in a South-Eastern Mexican community: impacts of male labour migration on the women left behind', *Mobilities*, 7, 3, pp. 369–88.

Philippine Statistics Authority (2019) *Statistical Tables on Overseas Filipino Workers* (OFW): 2017. Available at https://tinyurl.com/yywjgkev (last accessed 2/9/2019).

Rawlence, B. (2016) *City of Thorns: Nine lives in the world's largest refugee camp.* London: Portobello Books.

UNHCR (2019) *Dadaab Refugee Complex.* Available online at https://tinyurl.com/yyfq3tsv (last accessed 2/9/2019).

US Department of Agriculture (2019) *Farm Labor.* Available at https://tinyurl.com/y2jcu9zb (last accessed 2/9/2019).

Wahba, J. (2019) 'Why Syrian refugees have no negative effects on Jordan's labour market', *The Conversation*, 2 September. Available at https://tinyurl.com/y5u9dzm4 (last accessed 14/9/2019).

Younge, G. (2018) 'The NHS, Windrush and the debt we owe to immigration', *The Guardian*, 22 June. Available at https://tinyurl.com/y7c8exph (last accessed 14/9/2019).

ACTIVITY BOX 5

'Dadaab Stories' (www.dadaabstories.org) shows films made by refugees living in the Dadaab refugee camp in Kenya.

1a Watch at least two of the films from the Camp Life or Camp Services sections.
1b Draw a spider diagram showing how the camp tries to keep residents safe and some of the challenges that they face in meeting the security requirements.
1c How far do the films support your existing views on life in refugee camps?
2a Using data from the KNOMAD website (www.knomad.org) select three countries from different regions of the world and write a short description of their migration and remittances profile.
2b Compare and contrast the profiles of the three countries.
2c To what extent are brain drain, brain gain and brain circulation useful concepts for explaining the impacts of migration in these countries?
3a Review your Venn diagram from Activity Box 3. Use the ideas and examples in this chapter to annotate and illustrate the reasons why migration is limited, and why it should not be limited.
3b To what extent do these annotations help explain the obligations that countries have signed up to (overlap of Venn diagram)?

Extra resources to accompany this chapter are available on the Top Spec web pages.
See page 4 for further information.

6. The contested nature of migration

As described in Chapter 5, migration has consequences for source and host countries at a range of scales. However, different groups respond to these consequences in different ways, which change over time as political movements ebb and flow. This chapter will examine how patterns of migration are subject to different interpretations – nationalist, transnationalist, multiculturalist, and populist – and explore contemporary representations of migration in the USA, Mexico, the Philippines and Eritrea.

Interpreting the consequences of migration

Nationalism

Nationalism inspires loyalty to the institutions and ideals of the nation-state, through symbols and historical allegories. Symbols of nationalism such as flags, works of art, national anthems, architecture and physical landmarks reinforce a sense of national consciousness. A shared affection for these symbols reinforces a sense of community and pride in the achievements and culture of the nation. Legal systems and methods of governance are also linked to national identity. Many Americans revere their democracy as part of their identity and talk about their nation being 'the land of the free and the home of the brave' (Oxford Bibliographies, 2016).

National separations run counter to globalisation, in a world where economic and social activity routinely crosses national borders. Chapter 3 explained the legal background to border controls and free movement. The 20th century's two world wars were driven in part by nationalism. Co-operation across national borders, in the form of the UN and the EU, was established in the aftermath of these conflicts. The aim of such organisations was to demonstrate that co-operation between states could generate better outcomes than competition between them.

Most developed economies are now tightly interconnected with the global economy; most developing economies are also becoming increasingly interconnected. Processes of migration over many decades have made many states multi-ethnic. Questions of national identity and loyalty have become complex: a modern nationalism might represent diversity as a source of strength and an ideal of the nation-state. An example of this would be the opening ceremony of the 2012 Olympic Games in London, a showpiece event that celebrated Britain's diversity and proclaimed it as a strength. However, modern nationalism can also represent exclusion; recent migrants can be regarded as outside the shared national consciousness.

INFORMATION BOX 6.1 NATION, STATE, NATION-STATE

A nation is commonly defined as a large group of people, generally linked by common descent, historical and possibly linguistic ties, having common interests of place and land. This is distinct from a state, which refers to the political organisation forming the basis of civil government. A nation-state unifies these terms, and refers to a sovereign state most of whose members constitute a nation. (Clark, 1998)

Figure 6.1 The last night of the Proms, Albert Hall, London. Waving a flag is a common use of a national symbol to express national identity. **Photo:** © Homer Sykes/Alamy Stock Photo.

INFORMATION BOX 6.2
WHITE NATIONALISM

White nationalism is not the same as nationalism. Nation-states and their traditions create the basis for nationalism. These places exist and their traditions can be defined. White nationalists want to create an ethno-state of whites. Ethnicity is the key factor; many white nationalists believe that races form a hierarchy with white people at the top (*Economist*, 2019).

Figure 6.2 White nationalists and counter-protesters clash during a white nationalist rally at Charlottesville, VA, on 12 August 2017 that turned violent, resulting in one death and multiple injuries. **Photo:** © Kim Kelley-Wagner/Shutterstock.

Transnationalism

Transnationalism has its origins in efforts to organise manufacturing production in the most efficient and profitable manner, regardless of political boundaries. The idea emerged in the aftermath of the First World War and can be seen in part as a response to the failures of nationalism. Multinational corporations are an example of economic transnationalism. Over time, individuals, companies and institutions have established links across national borders. As these relationships have deepened, transnationalism has gained a meaning that goes beyond economics (Willis, 2014). In the modern world, some transnationalists argue that it does not make sense to hinder the global movement of capital, goods, services, workers, ideas and scientific co-operation. These ideas are popular among some capitalists. They promote free trade, unhindered by government regulation and tariffs. Others, who are more critical of capitalism, in particular what they regard as its negative environmental and social externalities, promote transnational organisations to regulate our interconnected world: firstly, to resolve those problems, such as climate change and plastic pollution, that go beyond national boundaries; secondly, to maximise and maintain opportunities for individuals and communities to benefit from global interconnections.

Both groups see migration as a necessary and desirable process. This might be the movement of labour, to ensure the most efficient allocation of resources in the capitalist system. It might be transnational activism and regulation in the face of global problems. Or it might be the right of individuals, families or the wider diaspora to choose where and how they live, without the hindrance of national borders.

Figure 6.3 The flags of the UN and EU in the European Council building, Brussels, Belgium. These intergovernmental organisations can be seen as examples of transnationalism in practice. **Photo:** © Alexandros Michailidis/Shutterstock.

Multiculturalism

Migrations over time have had the cumulative effect of increasing the size and number of diasporas, and this has led to the creation of multi-ethnic states. Imperial map-making also created multi-ethnic colonies, whose character survived the process of decolonisation. Multiculturalism interprets the consequences of migration as an opportunity to learn from and share with other cultures. This interpretation recognises that migration leads to cultural and ethnic change, but sees this as an enriching process. Professor Bhikhu Parekh, writing in the *Guardian* in January 2005, captured this interpretation:

> *No culture represents the last word in human wisdom. It articulates a particular vision of human life, develops a particular range of human capacities and emotions, and marginalises others ... Multiculturalism is not about shutting oneself up in a communal or cultural ghetto and leading a segregated and self-contained life. Rather it is about opening up oneself to others, learning from their insights and criticisms, growing as a result into a richer and tolerant culture.* (Parekh, 2005)

Multiculturalism is an umbrella term for a number of similar approaches to cultural change, including identity politics, the politics of recognition, national self-determination, multinational citizenship, secularism and religious diversity. All of these approaches advocate accommodating ethnic and cultural minorities within the cultural, public and legal institutions of the host nation. For example, linguistic and religious minorities might demand the right to operate their own separate religious schools with public funding. Other minorities may seek exemptions from certain regulations such as dress codes that inhibit their participation in public institutions (Oxford Bibliographies, 2016).

Multiculturalists agree that states should accommodate some of the demands of cultural minorities; however, they disagree about the precise nature of that accommodation. They also disagree about the extent to which the rights of minority groups should take priority if they conflict with broader concerns for freedom, equality and fundamental human rights. There are also debates about how to address the impact of multicultural policies on citizenship, social cohesion, and national unity.

Populism

Populism is the idea that society is separated into 'the people' and 'the elite'. 'The people' can be defined along class, ethnic or national lines. 'The elite' is the political, economic, cultural and media establishment, depicted as a homogeneous entity. Populists accuse the elite of placing their own interests, and/or the interests of foreign countries and immigrants, above the interests of 'the people' (Mudde, 2017).

This is not a new phenomenon. However, there has been a rise in populist movements since the 2008 Great Recession. A wealthy 'elite' of bankers and financiers were responsible for an economic crisis, the costs of which were borne by society at large. Austerity and economic stagnation, fears about the growth of artificial intelligence and robotisation allied to continuing globalisation and the use of social media to influence popular opinion, created a ready audience for populist messages. Populism is not the same as nationalism, but it catalyses unease in some social groups arising from a perceived challenge to their national identity.

Populism presents 'the people' as a homogeneous group. All individuals regarded as being 'native' to a particular state, either by birth

Figure 6.4 President Trump condemns what he calls the 'dishonest' media establishment during a speech at Harrisburg, Pennsylvania, USA in April 2017. **Photo:** © Evan El-Amin/Shutterstock.

or by ethnicity, can be considered part of 'the people' (Mudde, 2017). This necessarily excludes migrant communities from definitions of 'the people'. Those who advocate for the rights of minority groups or a migrant diaspora can be dismissed as part of 'the elite'. Moreover, populists argue that multinational companies and intergovernmental organisations, such as the UN and the EU, promote the agenda of 'the elite' and are the enemy of 'the people'. This fits with a broad opposition to immigration, as these organisations are often the strongest advocates for and prominent examples of transnationalism.

Contemporary representations of migration

Nationalism: Eritrea

Eritrea is one of the world's youngest countries, established by the UN in 1952 as an autonomous region within the Ethiopian–Eritrean Federation. In 1962 Ethiopia annexed Eritrea as a province, starting 30 years of violence as Eritrea fought to regain its independence, and in 1991 Eritrean rebels finally defeated the Ethiopian government forces. Independence from Ethiopia was overwhelmingly approved in a 1993 UN-supervised referendum and Eritrea was admitted to the UN the same year. Isaias Afwerki has been Eritrea's president ever since: Eritrea is a one-party state, and there have been no elections since the referendum. Afwerki's regime is run on nationalist lines, emphasising nationalist symbols and loyalties. Eritrean society is highly militarised, and national military and civilian service of indefinite length is mandatory. Afwerki's rule has become increasingly autocratic and repressive.

80% of the Eritrean workforce are employed in agriculture (Jordan, 2016), but farming fails to meet the needs of Eritrea's growing population. Drought, overgrazing and soil erosion are persistent problems, exacerbated by a labour shortage due to conscription, and because the government prioritises defence spending over agriculture. The long war for independence also damaged Eritrea's economy. As a result, since at least the 1960s, Eritrea has been a leading source country for migration to Sudan, Ethiopia, Yemen, Egypt and Israel. This large diaspora has been a source of vital remittances, funding its war for independence and providing 30% of the country's GDP annually since it became independent. Young people fleeing the country to avoid conscription face strict exit controls and limited access to travel documents, making them vulnerable to trafficking (CIA World Factbook, 2019).

INFORMATION BOX 6.3
EAST AFRICA

While it is true that Eritrea experiences poor government and that many of its people live hard lives, it is important to recognise that economic, social and political progress is being made in East Africa. For example, the region is seeing the fastest economic growth on the continent (African Development Bank, 2019). Kenya began exporting crude oil in 2019. (Mpungu, 2019).

Transnationalism: the USA

Transnationalists argue that historical links between peoples across national borders explain patterns of migration better than abstract economic principles. For example, the USA has historical connections with China (Chinese migrants were recruited in the 1860s for the construction of the Pacific Railroad) that explain the location and size of the Chinese diaspora in the USA. The USA also has historical connections to the Philippines (colonisation prior to the Second World War; conquest during the war, and post-war governance) that explain the extent of the American diaspora in the Philippines and the Filipino diaspora in the USA. Foreign direct investment (FDI) by US companies in Mexico and the historical provision of Latino labour in the south western USA explain the depth of migration and integration between these two countries. Nations much poorer than the USA have not experienced the same migration flows or diaspora: the push and pull factors may be similar for Mongolians as for Filipinos, but the extent of their historical interconnection is not (Wikipedia, 2019a).

Transnationalists would also argue that the process of globalisation has itself created the flows of migration that we see today. Multinational organisations have relocated manufacturing industry from OECD countries to emerging economies. This has transformed the structure of OECD economies, which are now predominantly service industry-based, with a mixture of very well-paid, high-skilled jobs and a larger number of lower-paid, low-skilled jobs. The well-paid workers create the demand for services, the provision of which requires immigration to fill the lower-paid, low-skilled jobs. The impact of FDI inside emerging economies has been to drive rural-urban migration; within a generation, the increased earnings potential of higher productivity work leads to broader participation in education, empowering the young to migrate to the countries whose multinationals provided the FDI in the first place.

While transnationalists argue that migration generates greater prosperity on an aggregate, per capita and per worker basis, populists argue that this only benefits the elite, because the costs and benefits of this growth are not evenly distributed (Goldin et al., 2018). Populist parties and social movements are often led by charismatic figures who present themselves as 'the voice of the people'. Marine Le Pen in France, Viktor Orbán in Hungary, Rodrigo Duterte in the Philippines and Donald Trump in the USA all combine populism with anti-immigrant nativism and authoritarianism. To distance themselves from the establishment and retain their status as a challenge to 'the elite' they do not behave like traditional politicians: they refuse to accept conventions, they are constantly campaigning, and sometimes they give utterance to outrageous claims.

The United States of America has seen many waves of migration since its foundation. Over time, these waves of migrants have come to be accepted as Americans, and many argue that there is no reason why new ethnic groups cannot be as successfully integrated. As a result, multiculturalism in America has now developed into two strands. The first proposes that the USA is a country in which many diverse cultures can co-exist and find common ground as Americans. This captures something of the American dream: that anyone, regardless of their origins, can succeed in the USA. The second strand, which perhaps explains the success of populist movements in the USA, is more contested: it argues that people derive their primary identities from their racial or ethnic groups. In this view the role of the government is not only to accept integration but also to facilitate it (Renshon and Renshon, 2011).

Multiculturalism: Mexico

In Mexico, too, history supports multiculturalism. In 2014 the Council of Europe ranked Mexico City 13th out of 59 world cities – the highest rank outside Europe – in terms of its multiculturalism and how effectively its government improves diversity and cultural interaction (Council of Europe, 2014). The largest ethnic group in Mexico are the Mestizos, followed by indigenous Mexicans, then smaller ethnic groups such as Arab Mexicans, Afro-Mexicans, Asian Mexicans and White Mexicans (those of European extraction). Historically, Mestizos are half-Spanish and half-indigenous, a consequence of the Spanish conquest of the Aztec empire in the 16th century. A key characteristic of Mexican culture, therefore, is its *mestizaje* – the intermixing of Spanish and indigenous roots and adaptation to the cultural traditions of immigrants. Despite Mexico's promotion of diversity and interaction, many indigenous groups are marginalised. In the decade to 2010, the number of people in Mexico who had been born in another country – mostly Guatemala and the USA – doubled, reaching almost 1 million (Wikipedia, 2019b).

Populism: the Philippines and the USA

The Philippines and the USA offer contrasting examples of how populists can use migration to campaign on behalf of the people against the elite. The Philippines has seen large migration flows to

Figure 6.5 Newly arrived European immigrants at Ellis Island, New York in 1920–21. **Photo:** © Everett Historical/Shutterstock.

the Middle East, often as domestic labour. This brings benefits to Filipinos, in particular through remittances, but such workers have always been vulnerable to exploitation. In this context 'the people' are the Filipino workers and 'the elite' are the Middle Eastern employers. In 2018, Philippine President Rodrigo Duterte threatened to cut off the flow of Filipino workers to the Middle East in response to incidents of rape and suicides of Filipinos in the region. Earlier in the year he suspended the issue of overseas work visas for Filipino nationals to work in Kuwait while the unexplained death of seven Filipino workers was investigated (Human Rights Watch, 2018). President Duterte uses migration as a tool to campaign for an identified people against a seemingly corrupt elite.

One of President Trump's campaign promises was to build a wall to prevent migration across the southern border of the USA; he also promised to make Mexico pay to build the wall. In this case, Trump defines 'the people' as Americans whose living standards and security are undermined by migration. The 'elite' are those who benefit from migrant labour – wealthy households that employ cleaners and au pairs, for instance. In the USA, 17.2% of household workers are migrants (ILO, 2015).

This interpretation can be seen in a speech that President Trump gave in January 2019, as reported by the BBC:

If a wall is immoral, why do wealthy politicians build walls, fences and gates around their homes? (BBC, 2019)

This migration narrative reinforces President Trump's persona as the voice of the people, even though his own wealth and occupation would identify him as part of the elite.

Figure 6.6 Demonstrators at Tijuana, Baja California, on the Mexican side of the border before the arrival of President Trump to inspect plans for the wall in March 2018. **Photo:** © AlejandroGutierrez/Shutterstock.

References

African Development Bank (2019) *East Africa's economy races ahead of its African peers, modest growth forecast for the rest of the continent.* Available at https://tinyurl.com/y2stwpju (last accessed 29/8/2019).

BBC (2019) *Why does Donald Trump want to build a wall?* Available at www.bbc.co.uk/newsround/46811167 (last accessed 29/8/2019).

CIA World Factbook (2019) *Country Profiles.* Available at https://tinyurl.com/y3hurcgs (last accessed 24/8/2019).

Clark, A. (1998) *Dictionary of Geography*, (2nd edition). London: Penguin Books.

Council of Europe (2014) *Mexico City: Results of the Intercultural Cities Index.* Available at https://tinyurl.com/y69pkrc2 (last accessed 29/8/2019).

Economist (2019) *What is 'White Nationalism'?* Available at https://tinyurl.com/y2ws9uxx (last accessed 29/8/2019).

Goldin, I., Pitt, A., Nabarro, B. and Boyle, K. (2018) *Migration and the Economy.* Oxford: Citi GPS/Oxford Martin School. Available at https://tinyurl.com/y4emoe52..

Human Rights Watch (2018) *Duterte Threatens to Ban Labor Migration to the Middle East.* Available at https://tinyurl.com/y4wns5y8 (last accessed 29/8/2019).

ILO Labour Migration Branch (2015) *Global Estimates on Migrant Workers.* Geneva: ILO

Jordan, R. (2016) 'Eritrea: Farming in a fragile land', *Huffington Post*, 18 March.

Mpungu, P. (2019) 'Kenya joins ranks of oil-exporting countries', *Al Jazeera News*, 26 August. Available at https://tinyurl.com/yynd2qco (last accessed 6/10/2019).

Mudde, C. (2017) *Populism: A Very Short Introduction.* Oxford: Oxford University Press.

Oxford Bibliographies (2016) *Nationalism.* Available at https://tinyurl.com/yy2kd45o (last accessed 29/8/2019).

Parekh, B. (2005) 'Multiculturalism is a civilised dialogue', The *Guardian*, 21 January.

Renshon, S. and Renshon, S. (2011) *Multiculturalism in the U.S.: Cultural Narcissism and the Politics of Recognition.* Available at https://tinyurl.com/yyhr6bat (last accessed 29/8/2019).

Wikipedia (2019a) *Transnationalism.* Available at https://tinyurl.com/y3klm29o (last accessed 29/8/2019).

Wikipedia (2019b) *Multiculturalism.* Available at https://tinyurl.com/y4wnsovn (last accessed 29/8/2019).

Willis, K. (2014) 'Migration and transnationalism' in Desai, V. and Potter, R. (eds) (2014) *The Companion to Development Studies* (3rd edition). London: Routledge, pp. 212–16.

ACTIVITY BOX 6

1. Summarise the key characteristics of nationalism, multiculturalism, transnationalism and populism.
2. Identify the key differences between these doctrines.
3. Organise the doctrines on a spectrum ranging from pro-migration to anti-migration.
4. Review a broadsheet newspaper from your country: how many quotes in stories about migration can you find that correspond with each of the viewpoints?
5. Use this chapter and your own research to answer this exam question: 'Transnationalism best explains current attitudes to migration'. To what extent do you agree with this statement?

Extra resources to accompany this chapter are available on the Top Spec web pages. See page 4 for further information.

7. The fluidity of borders

Introduction

Maps make borders looked solid and immutable. In reality, borders can change over time, and this can have devastating consequences for the people thus displaced. For example, the 1947 partition of British India into the independent states of India and Pakistan resulted in 14–16 million people being displaced: Hindus living in what became Pakistan often moved to India and Muslims to Pakistan (Ansari, 2017). Borders also do not operate in the same way for everyone. For some groups and individuals borders may be very difficult, if not impossible, to cross; others may find it easy. This chapter explores the fluidity of borders.

Statelessness

According to the 1954 UN Convention relating to the Status of Stateless Persons, a stateless' person is a person who 'is not considered as a national by any state under the operation of its law' (UNHCR, 2019). In 2014, the Institute on Statelessness and Inclusion (ISI) estimated that there were more than 15 million stateless people in the world (ISI, 2014). Stateless people have no official documentation, so access to education, healthcare and employment, and crossing international borders, may be difficult or impossible.

Statelessness may come about because an individual never claimed, or was not able to claim, a nationality when they were born. Nationality is usually based either on parentage or place of birth, but countries vary as to which of these criteria is used. International migration has increased the possibility of being stuck between different systems. Some children born abroad to single mothers fleeing conflict in the Syrian Arab Republic have been left stateless. This is because children can only acquire Syrian nationality from their father. A child born in a country that does not confer nationality on all those born within its territory has no legal way to acquire a nationality (Osborne and Russell, 2015).

Changing borders may also contribute to statelessness. If national borders are redrawn, through a part of a state becoming independent, or a state dividing into a number of new states, some individuals or groups may be left stateless. For example, during the border conflict with Eritrea in 1998–2000, some Ethiopians of Eritrean origin were stripped of their Ethiopian nationality and expelled from the country. An estimated 150,000 individuals of Eritrean descent who remained in Ethiopia were not considered Ethiopians, but had not acquired another nationality.

UNHCR is committed to ending statelessness by 2024. This will involve encouraging governments to change laws to grant nationality to current stateless people, and to prevent statelessness in the future (UNHCR, 2019).

Borders: doors or walls?

In Chapter 3 we discussed the governance mechanisms states use to protect their borders and regulate who is allowed to come into the country and on what basis. The visa system is key to this. In 2018 there were over 190 million individual crossings from Mexico to the USA at the US-Mexico border, most of which were undertaken in a private

Figure 7.1 Cars at Tijuana, Mexico, waiting to pass into the USA.
Photo: © James Steidl/Shutterstock.

Figure 7.2 Road sign indicating the border between France and Belgium.
Photo: © defotoberg/Shutterstock.

vehicle (see Figure 7.3). Some of these crossings would be American citizens travelling back to the US after visiting or working in Mexico, but millions would be undertaken by non-US citizens. These individuals might cross the border frequently for business trips or to visit family, while others were tourists. Some cross-border travel will have been migration – people moving their place of residence for at least three months (see Chapter 3). In all cases, individuals will have been able to enter the USA legally either because of their nationality (US citizens) or because they have been granted a visa or visa waiver on the basis that the USA immigration authorities do not regard them as a threat, or perceive them as socially and economically beneficial to the USA.

For the nearly 400,000 people apprehended by the US Border Patrol in 2018 and identified as 'deportable aliens', the border is very solid. They are not US citizens, do not have visas and are not regarded as having a valid reason to enter the USA, so they are liable for deportation – return to their home countries. In 2018, just over 150,000 of the people apprehended were Mexican, approximately 115,000 were from Guatemala and about 31,400 were from El Salvador (US Customs and Border Protection, 2019).

Flexible citizenship
Aihwa Ong (1999) developed the concept of 'flexible citizenship' to describe how privileged migrants are able to successfully navigate national migration systems. She uses the example of Hong Kong migrants to the USA to show the links between economic globalisation, migration and identity. Political uncertainty due to the imminent handover of Hong Kong to China in 1997 caused wealthy Hong Kong businesspeople to consider moving their households to a more stable environment, and at the same time exploit the potential for foreign investment in the USA. The USA visa system allowed them to enter the country as entrepreneurs or investors, to set up a family home and in due course to take out US citizenship. The US government saw this as a way to attract foreign investment; for the Hong Kong migrants, there was security, and educational opportunities for their children. This type of migration often led to so-called 'astronaut families' where mothers and children lived in the USA, while fathers travelled backwards and forwards across the Pacific for business.

Unaccompanied children
In humanitarian terms, refugee status does not in most cases change over time. However, the case of unaccompanied children (or 'unaccompanied minors') demonstrates how borders that were porous can suddenly become solid. According to both the 1951 Refugee Convention and the United Nations 1989 Convention on the Rights of the Child, children (defined as people under the age of 18) should be given protection by states if they are travelling without family members. This protection only applies to children, so once an individual reaches the age of 18, they may not be legally eligible to stay in the host country and could be deported.

Since 1998 an estimated 15% of the population of Eritrea has fled the country to escape violence and insecurity. This flow has included unaccompanied young people escaping compulsory military service: in Eritrea this can last indefinitely, representing a form of slavery. Religious intolerance is also a push factor, for all ages. Only four religious groups are recognised by the Eritrean government, and members of other faiths may be persecuted (Human Rights Watch, 2019). In the context of the refugee flows into Europe since 2015 the plight of Syrians has received most attention, but in terms of unaccompanied children Eritreans are more prominent. In 2018 19,700 unaccompanied minors claimed asylum in member states of the EU. Of these, Eritreans made up 10%, exceeded only by Afghanis (16%) (Eurostat, 2019).

Host countries must accept unaccompanied children but are not obliged to grant them asylum when they reach 18. Children whose asylum applications fail can appeal, but if the appeal also fails they can be returned to their country of origin. Given the human rights situation in Eritrea, this is not likely to happen to Eritrean children in the near future; but it is the experience of young people from 'safe' countries, even if they have no family there, they have established a life in the host country and they still fear for their safety (Gladwell et al., 2016). One day a vulnerable child; the next, an adult, liable to be deported.

Internal borders
Migration governance can also be seen within countries. As described in Chapter 4, since the 1960s China has used the *hukou* or household registration system to control rural-urban migration. After coming to power in 1949, the Communist Party sought to restrict urbanisation and prevent potential resulting unrest,

Type of crossing	Number entering US[a]
Bus passengers	1,838,132
Pedestrians	46,173,881
Private vehicle passengers	144,891,237
Train passengers	10,436
Apprehended by US Border Patrol[b]	396,579

Figure 7.3 Mexico-US border crossings, 2018. **Sources:** (a) Bureau of Transportation Statistics (2019); (b) US Customs and Border Protection (2019).

overcrowding and poor conditions, by enhancing the existing registration system and preventing movement to the cities without a migration permit (Cheng and Selden, 1994). Since the 1980s and the opening up of the Chinese economy, rural–urban migration controls have been relaxed somewhat. However, access to services in the host province or city is controlled through the *hukou* system. If you do not have a local *hukou* then you will be excluded from access to health services, education and welfare. There may also be limits to your ability to access housing. This means that migrant workers from the countryside often leave their spouse (and children) in the rural areas, live in very basic conditions in the city and only return to the family home at Chinese New Year.

Maintaining international borders may also have an impact internally. As a way of both discouraging undocumented migration and apprehending individuals who have broken migration regulations, some countries require institutions or individuals to monitor the migration status of service users. For example, in the UK, universities sponsor international students to enter the country to study for their degree. If a student is not attending classes the university is legally obliged to report the fact to the Home Office, or face the possible removal of their sponsor status. Private landlords are also required to check tenants' documentation. This is a form of border policing, conducted not by border officials or law enforcement officers, but by other service providers (Cassidy, 2019).

Changes over time

The 1951 UNHCR Refugee Convention underpins the international system of refugee protection and the immigration laws and policies of signatory countries. As described in Chapter 3, the Convention identifies fear of persecution on the grounds of race, religion and nationality as being the basis of a claim for asylum. This reflects the context in which the Convention was written – the aftermath of the Second World War, and the persecution of some ethnic and religious groups, particularly by the Nazis. However, the Convention also identifies fear of persecution on the ground of 'membership of a particular social group' as a basis, opening up the possibility of individuals being able to claim refugee status due to fearing persecution based on a different characteristic.

LGBTQ+ refugees

As of early 2019 there were approximately 70 countries where homosexuality is criminalised, including some countries where it incurs the death penalty (Mendos, 2019). Gay men were targets of Nazi persecution, but sexual orientation was not included as a specific category in the 1951 Convention – not least because male homosexuality was in any case illegal in many Western countries at that time. However, in recent decades LGBTQ+ (lesbian, gay, bisexual, transgender, queer or questioning) individuals have successfully made asylum claims because their persecution is based on their 'membership of a particular social group' (Stonewall, 2019).

Climate refugees

Climate change is making lives and livelihoods increasingly difficult for millions of people. Water scarcity, falling crop yields due to drought, and more intense weather events, such as typhoons, means that it is increasingly difficult, especially in rural areas, for households to support themselves. In low-lying coastal regions, rising sea levels even threaten land to live on. These challenges have led to calls for a new category of 'climate refugee' to be recognised (Berchin et al., 2017), although so far no international organisation or national government has adopted it, not least because of the challenges of defining climate change as the main cause of migration and the potential size of migrant flows that could result.

In 2015 Ioane Teitiota, a citizen of Kiribati, a Pacific island nation, submitted an asylum claim to the New Zealand courts on the basis that returning to Kiribati would put him and his family at significant risk due to sea level rise. Following his unsuccessful claim Teitiota was deported (Hall, 2017).

Figure 7.4 Rainbow Refugees Munich attending a Gay Pride parade, July 2018. **Photo:** © WhiteHaven/Shutterstock.

The future of migration governance

The system of global governance set up after the Second World War has provided protection for millions of refugees and IDPs, and has also created a system of norms whereby states exert sovereignty over their territory through the control of their borders. However, in recent years, freedom of movement within this system has become more difficult: borders are more strictly policed, sometimes through the erection of physical barriers, such as President Trump's proposed border wall between the USA and Mexico (Marshall, 2018). These trends may be due to the rise of populism (see Chapter 6): citizens of host countries are increasingly concerned about immigration's perceived threat to their jobs and way of life. At the same time protectionism is on the rise; higher import tariffs and increased regulation are being imposed in an attempt to protect national industries.

Despite these changes, migration will continue. This may be because of the demand for workers to support ageing populations or the skills gaps that local workers or technology cannot fill. There will continue to be significant numbers of people fleeing persecution, conflict or extreme poverty, perhaps exacerbated by climate change. In an international state-based system, governance mechanisms will continue to be vital in providing a framework within which ongoing migration can be managed. As with current regulations and international treaties, there will be a lack of consistency, with supposedly universal rights being interpreted and implemented differently depending on location. However, it is likely that human rights and migrant organisations will continue to campaign for migration governance systems that operate to protect the rights of migrants regardless of the type of border and the characteristics of the migrants.

ACTIVITY BOX 7

1. Make two lists from this chapter: people for whom borders are fluid; people for whom borders are solid.
2. List the reasons given in this chapter why border controls may become more fluid or more solid.
3. State which categories of people in your original lists are most likely to be impacted by the reasons in the third list. Give your reasons.
4. Read Nina Hall's article in 'The Conversation' (https://tinyurl.com/yyutvlyk) about climate change refugees and summarise the challenges of making climate change a reason for humanitarian protection.
5. Watch the short film 'Hamedullah: The Road Home' by Sue Clayton (www.bigjourneys.org/archive) What examples of migration governance can you see in this film?

References

Ansari, S. (2017) 'How the Partition of India happened – and why its effects are still felt today', *The Conversation*, 10 August. Available at https://tinyurl.com/y63urws7 (last accessed 5/10/2019).

Berchin, I.B., Valduga, I.B., Garcia, J., Salgueirinho, J.B. and de Andrade Guerra, O. (2017) 'Climate change and forced migrations: an effort towards recognizing climate refugees', *Geoforum*, 84, pp. 147–50.

Bureau of Transportation Statistics (2019) *Border Crossing/Entry Data*. Available at www.bts.gov/content/border-crossingentry-data (last accessed 7/9/2019).

Cassidy, K. (2019) 'Everyday bordering: the internal reach of the UK's borders', *Geography*, 104, 2, pp. 100–102.

Cheng, T. and Selden, M. (1994) 'The origins and social consequences of China's Hukou system', *The China Quarterly*, 139, pp. 644–68.

Eurostat (2019) 'Almost 20,000 unaccompanied minors among asylum seekers registered in the EU in 2018'. Eurostat News Release 73/2019, 26 April. Available at https://tinyurl.com/y3tawz9w (last accessed 24/9/2019).

Gladwell, C., Bowerman, E., Norman, B. and Dickson, S., with Ghafoor, A. (2016) *After Return: Documenting the experiences of young people forcibly removed to Afghanistan*. London: Refugee Support Network. Available at https://tinyurl.com/y5gatwbu (last accessed 24/9/2019).

Hall, N. (2017) *Six things New Zealand's new government needs to do to make climate refugee visas work*, The Conversation, 30 November. Available at https://tinyurl.com/yyutvlyk (last accessed 24/9/2019).

Human Rights Watch (2019) *World Report 2019*. Available at www.hrw.org/world-report/2019 (last accessed 24/9/2019).

ISI (2014) *The World's Stateless*. Oisterwijk: Wolf Legal Publishers. Available at https://tinyurl.com/y498gcd7 (last accessed 24/9/2019).

Marshall, T. (2018) *Divided: Why we are living in an age of walls*. London: Elliott and Thompson Ltd.

Mendos, L.R. (2019) *State-sponsored Homophobia 2019*. Geneva: ILGA. Available at https://tinyurl.com/yypzthkn (last accessed 7/10/2019).

Ong, A. (1999) *Flexible Citizenship: The cultural logics of transnationality*. Durham, NC: Duke University Press.

Osborne, L. and Russell, R. (2015) 'Stateless in Europe: "We are no people with no nation"', *The Guardian*, 27 December. Available at https://tinyurl.com/y3fg6czv (last accessed 5/10/2019).

Stonewall (2019) *An Overview of Asylum*. Available at https://tinyurl.com/y22m7n94 (last accessed 24/9/2019).

UNHCR (2019) 'Ending statelessness'. Available at www.unhcr.org/uk/ending-statelessness.html (last accessed 3/9/2019).

US Customs and Border Protection (2019) 'US Border Patrol Apprehensions by Citizenship and Sector 2007–2018'. Available at https://tinyurl.com/y2dorty5 (last accessed 24/9/2019).

Extra resources to accompany this chapter are available on the Top Spec web pages. See page 4 for further information.

Key terms

Amnesty: a general pardon, usually by a government, of a particular group of people, for a specific offence.

Asset grab: to take advantage of weak regulations to obtain land, natural resources, property or industrial facilities for personal or corporate gain, often with detrimental impacts on wider economic growth.

Asylum: to seek asylum is to ask for the protection of a foreign government when fleeing war or persecution.

Autonomy: the ability to act independently.

Border: a legally significant demarcation line between countries, provinces, counties or local government districts.

Brain drain: the movement of the most highly skilled technical and professional people from the country where they trained and gained their first work experience to another offering better career opportunities and/or higher remuneration.

Citizenship: the legal status of being a citizen of a particular country with the rights and responsibilities that come with that status.

Contested: the subject of dispute or argument.

Decolonisation: the action or process of a state withdrawing from a former colony, making it independent.

Demographic dividend: the benefit to a country of a large population of working age.

Demographics: data relating to the size and characteristics of a population.

Dependency ratio: the ratio of the number of people not gainfully employed in a population (the dependents) to the number who are actively employed or potentially employable.

Deportation: the removal from a country of an individual who has no legal right to be there.

Diaspora: a group of people who have been, or whose ancestors were, dispersed from their original homeland.

Externality: a social, economic or environmental cost or benefit caused by the activity of an individual (or an institution) that does not enter the internal production costs of that activity but affects the activity of another (or others) and over which the latter has/have no control. A negative externality would be the plastic pollution caused by single use drinking water bottles. A positive externality would be if bees kept for honey pollinated crops in the surrounding fields.

Failed state: a state whose government is unable to perform the basic roles of a state, particularly in relation to security.

Flow (of migration): the number of migrants entering and leaving a country (inflow and outflow) over the course of a specific period, such as one year.

Food insecurity: insufficient healthy food on a day-to-day basis.

Foreign direct investment (FDI): an investment or controlling interest in a business by a foreign entity; investment in a country originating from outside that country.

Global city: a city that dominates global business. In 2018 the top ten global cities were London, New York, Tokyo, Paris, Singapore, Amsterdam, Seoul, Berlin, Hong Kong and Sydney.

Globalisation: the economic interdependence of countries worldwide through increasing volume and variety of cross-border transactions in goods and services, international capital flows, and diffusion of technology.

Governance: rule-making and regulation. This can be done by governments, multilateral organisations, companies or other institutions.

Gross domestic product (GDP): the value of all the goods and services a country produces.

Host country: the country to which an immigrant has come.

Human development index (HDI): a summary measure of a country's average achievement in key dimensions of human development: a long and healthy life, knowledge, and a decent standard of living.

Indigenous: belonging to the country in which they are found, rather than coming, or being brought, from another country.

Irregular migration: migration that takes place outside the regulatory norms of the source, transit and host country; also called 'undocumented migration'.

Latin America: a cultural, rather than a geographical, entity, which refers to countries in the Americas and the Caribbean where Spanish, Portuguese or French are the prevalent languages: Mexico, most of Central and South America, Cuba, the Dominican Republic, Haiti, and Puerto Rico.

Latino/Latina: a term used in the USA to describe a person who is, or is descended from, Latin Americans.

Median: the value separating the higher half from the lower half of a data sample.

Multiculturalism: an approach which recognises the value of cultural diversity and promotes understanding between different cultural or ethnic groups.

Multilateral: involving more than two nation-states, usually used to describe organisations such as the UN or EU.

Multiplier effect: when expenditure generates a greater increase in income and consumption than the initial amount spent.

Nationalism: loyalty and devotion to a particular nation, often implying a belief in the superiority of this nation to all others.

Nation-state: a sovereign state where most of the population share a common descent and historical or linguistic ties.

Nativism: the policy of favouring the natives of a country over immigrants.

Official development assistance (ODA): financial flows by official agencies, including state and local governments, into developing countries. These flows are intended to support economic development and welfare, and are concessional in character, with a grant element of at least 25%.

Organisation for Economic Co-operation and Development (OECD): a multilateral organisation promoting economic growth and democracy. Its members are largely high-income and very high HDI countries.

Peri-urban: an area of land immediately adjoining a city.

Population pyramid: a graph showing the distribution of age groups and gender in a population.

Populism: a political approach based on a distinction between 'ordinary people' and 'the elite'. Populism claims to support and represent the 'ordinary people'.

Primary city: a primary or primate city (from the Latin for 'prime' or 'first rank') is the largest city in its country or region, and is disproportionately larger than any others.

Primary industry: the extraction and collection of raw materials, such as coal and timber, and natural resources, such as fish, and agriculture. Developing countries tend to rely heavily on primary industries. **Secondary industries** take the output of primary industries to manufacture finished goods for export or the domestic market. **Tertiary industries** comprise services to primary and secondary industries and the community, e.g. financial services, education, transport and communications and the professions. The **quaternary sector** comprises intellectual and knowledge-based activities, research and administration.

Productivity: a ratio of a volume measure of output to a volume measure of input use.

Protectionism: the implementation of rules which make importing goods and services more expensive and difficult in order to protect domestic production.

Proxy war: an armed conflict between combatants acting on the instigation of other parties not directly involved in the hostilities.

Quaternary sector (see **Primary industry**).

Remittance: the money or goods that migrants send back to families and friends in source countries.

Secondary industry (see **Primary industry**).

Secularism: the separation of religious institutions and the state.

Source country: the country from which an immigrant has come.

Sovereignty: the authority of a state to rule over its territory and the people within its borders, without external interference.

Stateless: a person who is not considered a national by any state under the operation of its law.

Tertiary industry (see **Primary industry**).

Trafficking: recruiting and transporting people, through deception or coercion, for an improper purpose, e.g. forced labour or sexual exploitation.

Transnationalism: relationships and interactions that take place on a recurrent basis across international borders, by individuals, companies or organisations.

Visa: an official document, or a stamp put in your passport, which allows you to enter or leave a particular country.

Welfare state: social support provided by governments, typically free or subsidised healthcare, pensions, unemployment benefit and sick pay.

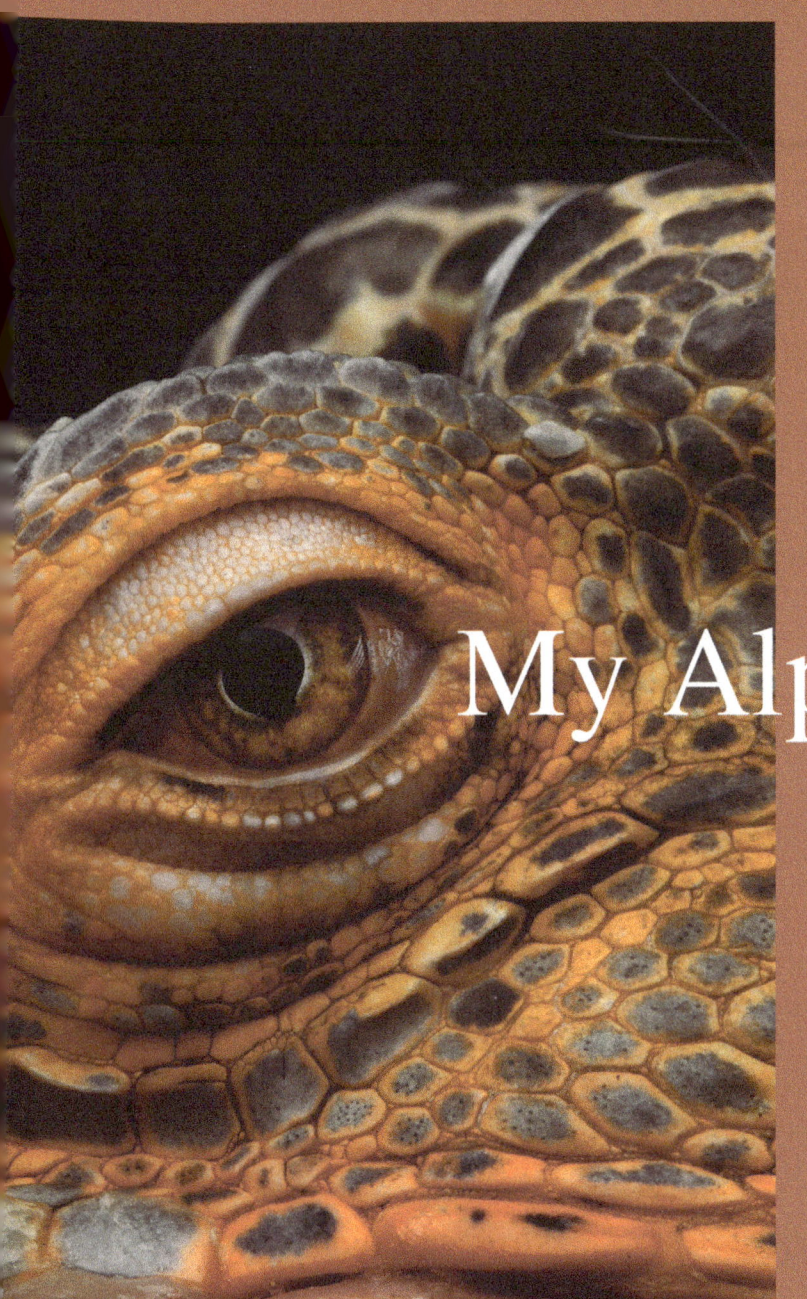

My Alphabetasaurus

Peter Winn

All rights reserved
Copyright © Peter Winn, 2022

The right of Peter Winn to be identified as the author of this
work has been asserted in accordance with Section 78
of the Copyright, Designs and Patents Act 1988

The book cover is copyright to Peter Winn

This book is published by
Grosvenor House Publishing Ltd
Link House
140 The Broadway, Tolworth, Surrey, KT6 7HT.
www.grosvenorhousepublishing.co.uk

This book is sold subject to the conditions that it shall not, by way of
trade or otherwise, be lent, resold, hired out or otherwise circulated
without the author's or publisher's prior consent in any form of binding or
cover other than that in which it is published and
without a similar condition including this condition being imposed
on the subsequent purchaser.

A CIP record for this book
is available from the British Library

ISBN 978-1-80381-249-6

To Mason
Happy 7th Birthday
from
Peter.

Introduction

If asked to work our way through the alphabet, how many could name a dinosaur for each letter. I suspect few of us could do this.

A recent survey I read showed that the five top favourites among youngsters were: Brachiosaurus, Velociraptor, Tyrannosaurus Rex, Stegosaurus and Triceratops. With T-Rex the clear winner!

The recent flood of dinosaur movies has shown us breath taking images of the most amazing creatures that ever walked on the land, swam the oceans, or flew the skies of our planet. Thousands of books have been written and the internet is a dinosaur lover's treasure trove.

It is estimated that more than eight hundred and fifty species of dinosaur have so far been discovered. Dubbed the "golden age of palaeontology," according to the National Geographic, there have been more than forty-five new dinosaur species discovered every year since 2003. No doubt many more will be discovered, especially in Asia.

So, back to the alphabet and our list. How many of us would have selected a dinosaur starting with the letter K – there are at least eighteen! More than forty dinosaur names start with the letter M and ten more begin with U. The letters X, Y and Z account for over thirty! We can thank China for many of the names starting with X and Y. According to The Natural History Museum in London over fifty species have so far been discovered in Asia, including Xiongguanlong, and Yutyrannous (featured in this book).

Included in this work are illustrations of dinosaurs covering all letters of the alphabet – however there are not twenty-six there are thirty, why?

Those of us who watched *Jurassic Park – The Lost World*, may remember seeing a group of inexperienced hunters attempting to lasso a Parasaurolophus – try saying that with a mouthful of wine gums! The magnificent, crested herbivore decided to turn its captors into unwilling merry-go-round riders when it swung them around while they desperately held onto the ropes attached to its crest. Well, Parasaurolophus is represented, but I could not leave out another P – Pachycephalosaurus, the bone-headed nutcase who frantically ran around head-butting anything that moved!

Allosaurus is joined by the living tank that is Ankylosaurus in representing A. Pachycephalosaurus and Parasaurolophus share the letter P. I also felt that the terrifying giant Spinosaurus should share the light with Stegosaurus under S and both Tyrannosaurus Rex and Triceratops fill the T slot.

In the image section of the book, you will note that the names of the dinosaurs are shown in one of three colours namely:

Red, showing the dinosaur to be a carnivore or meat-eater, Green which means the dinosaur is a herbivore or plant-eater and omnivore, who ate a variety of small animals, worms, grubs, seeds, fruit, and vegetation are shown in Brown.

I trust My Alphabetasaurus will be of interest and encourage readers to further investigate the magnificent Age of Dinosaurs.

Peter Winn

Contents

- Introduction — 1
- Continental Drift – Birth of the Earth — 5
- Age of Dinosaurs — 6
- Mesozoic Life on Land — 7
- Mesozoic Life in The Skies — 8
- Mesozoic Life in The Oceans — 9
- Mesozoic Plants and Trees — 10
- The Dinosaurs — 11
- Glossary — 42

CONTINENTAL DRIFT

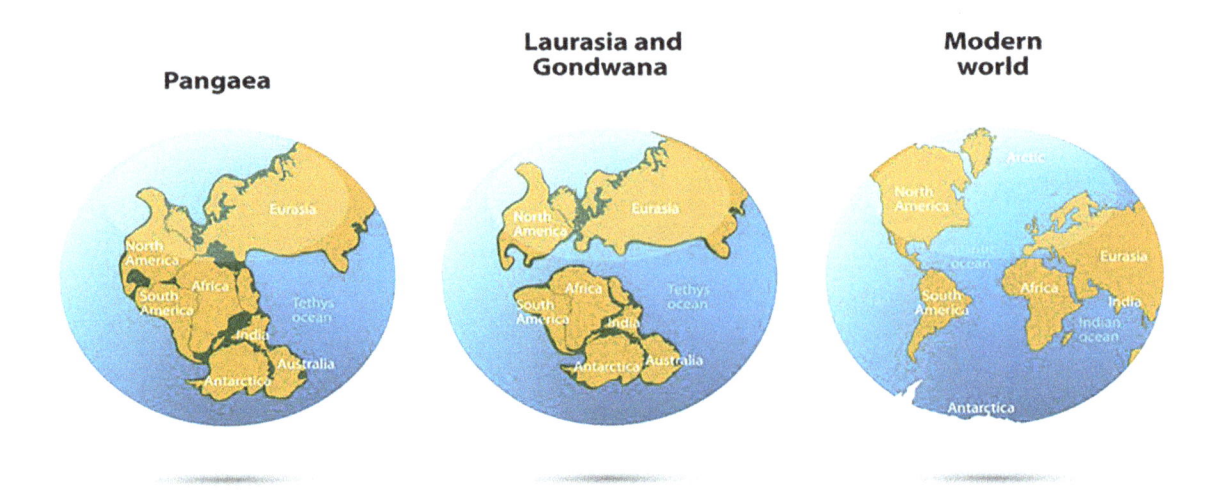

Pangaea **Laurasia and Gondwana** **Modern world**

Birth of the Earth

At the time of the **Triassic** Period the Earth was one massive continent named *Pangea – All Earth* – surrounded by an enormous ocean *Panthalassa – All Water*. There were no polar icecaps and the climate at the equator was hot and dry, with an average air temperature of 37 degrees Celsius. Conditions were wetter in the north and south.

The Jurassic Period saw Pangea split into two smaller continents, *Gondwana* in the south – comprising what are now Africa, South America, Australia and Antarctica, and *Laurasia* - including modern Europe, Asia, and North America in the north. As this happened huge lakes and rivers formed opening new ways for aquatic and terrestrial life to evolve.

During the **Cretaceous** Period, the breakup of the super-continents Gondwana and Laurasia continued and the first outlines of modern-day North and South America, Europe, Asia, and Africa began to take shape, and India first appeared as an island in the Tethys Ocean. Conditions continued hot and humid; sea levels rose creating endless swamps in which life would thrive.

Age of Dinosaurs

Dinosaurs were the dominant animals on Earth for over 160 million years. They remain the most successful life form to have ever roamed the planet. Dinosaurs adapted to and survived the violent and dramatic changes to the Earth's climatic and physical formation for longer than any other creature since their extinction.

In 1841, Richard Owen, the first director of London's Natural History Museum, gave the name **DINOSAUR** – *terrible lizard* to these prehistoric reptiles. The word dinosaur is from the Greek language for *deinos* – terrible- and *sauros* – lizard.

The last non-avian dinosaurs became extinct sixty-six million years ago. From the remains so far discovered, scientists know that dinosaurs are the prehistoric ancestors of today's crocodiles, snakes, and lizards.

Scientists also believe that modern birds are descended from dinosaurs.

During the **MESOZOIC** or *Middle Life Era*, animals changed rapidly. Reptiles, dinosaurs, fish, and mammals roamed the land, swam the oceans, and flew the skies from the Triassic period to the end of the Cretaceous period.

The Mesozoic is separated into three distinct periods.

The *Triassic Period* which lasted from 237 to 201 million years ago,
The *Jurassic Period*, from 201 to 145 million years ago, and
The *Cretaceous Period* from 145 to 66 million years ago.

Mesozoic Life on Land

The Triassic Period saw the emergence of the first crocodiles, dinosaurs, and early mammals. The development of these animals continued for millions of years into the Jurassic Period which brought about the greatest variety of land species of the whole Mesozoic Era. Brachiosaurus and Diplodocus and the medium to large-sized theropods such as Allosaurus and Megalosaurus first appeared and the first armoured dinosaurs like Ankylosaurus and Stegosaurus appeared.

The first feathered dinosaurs arrived, such as Archaeopteryx and Khaan. The mouse-sized early mammals of the Jurassic did their best to avoid being squashed or eaten by their dinosaur neighbours by feeding at night, and nesting deep in burrows or high in the trees! Dinosaurs ruled the Cretaceous. Over a period of eighty million years thousands of theropods roamed the slowly separating continents. These included raptors, tyrannosaurs and ornithomimids. The huge herbivores of the Jurassic had all but died out. Their descendants, the lightly armoured titanosaurs, spread to every continent and grew to massive proportions.

Mesozoic Life in the Skies

Pterosaurs were the first vertebrate creatures to conquer the air, long before birds took wing.
They ruled the skies for more than 160 million years before vanishing along with the
non-avian dinosaurs at the end of the Cretaceous period.
The smallest of these predators was the size of a sparrow.
The largest had a wingspan of ten metres!
Many possessed heads larger than their bodies, making them flying jaws of death.
Pterosaurs patrolled every ocean and continent on Earth. No animal in the Mesozoic would
have been safe from their hungry, searching eyes.
Birds, or avian dinosaurs, lived during the Mesozoic, the era when dinosaurs ruled the Earth.
Although researchers have discovered numerous Mesozoic bird species,
these were virtually all the size of crows or smaller,
Although one species grew as large as an ostrich!

Mesozoic Life in the Oceans

Panthalassa was perfect for the evolution of early marine reptiles,
including plesiosaurs and ichthyosaurs. Certain species of ichthyosaur
grew to a huge size – up to fifteen metres long and weighing thirty tonnes!

Soon Panthalassa became the home of prehistoric fish, octopus, squid,
cuttlefish, and corals.

Many marine reptiles of the Jurassic period grew to shark and whale-size,
and the seas were abundant with prehistoric fish, squids, and sharks,
thus providing a steady supply of food for these fearsome reptiles.

During the early Cretaceous period, the ichthyosaurs died out to be replaced by
vicious mosasaurs, gigantic predatory pliosaurs and smaller plesiosaurs.
Along with these reptiles evolved new breeds of bony fish and ancient sharks.

No place to go swimming!

Mesozoic Plants and Trees

The Triassic Period was not as lush and green as the later Jurassic and Cretaceous periods; the climate was too dry and much of Pangea was desert. Nevertheless, it saw the development of plants such as cycads, ferns, and mosses.

At the time of the Jurassic Period, Gondwana and Laurasia were covered with a blanket of thick vegetation and dense forests sporting ferns, conifers, cycads, and mosses. Plants continued their evolution, altogether providing vast amounts of food for the huge herbivores.

The Cretaceous is characterized by a revolution in the plant life, with the sudden appearance of flowering plants such as the ancestors of the beech, fig, magnolia, and sassafras. By the end of the Cretaceous such plants became dominant. It is interesting to note that the earliest verified grass fossils are from about fifty-five million years ago.

A a

Allosaurus

Pronounced: *Al-oh-sore-uss*

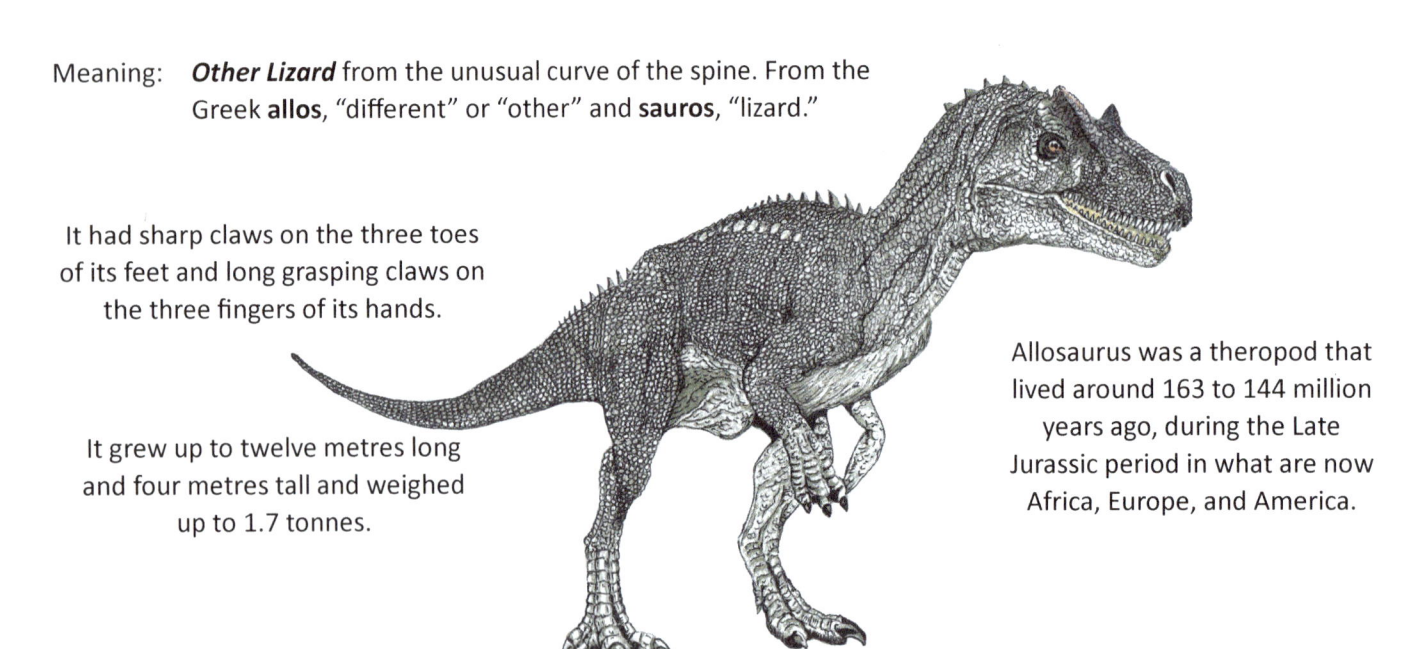

Meaning: **Other Lizard** from the unusual curve of the spine. From the Greek **allos**, "different" or "other" and **sauros**, "lizard."

It had sharp claws on the three toes of its feet and long grasping claws on the three fingers of its hands.

It grew up to twelve metres long and four metres tall and weighed up to 1.7 tonnes.

Allosaurus was a theropod that lived around 163 to 144 million years ago, during the Late Jurassic period in what are now Africa, Europe, and America.

Allosaurus was a top predator that roamed semi-dry floodplains and forests where it preyed on large herbivores such as Stegosaurus.

Allosaurus fossils have been found with puncture wounds matching those of a Stegosaurus tail-spike.

Also, some Stegosaurus fossils have been discovered with Allosaurus bite-marks.

The long, heavy tail helped the animal balance itself.

Scientists believe that Allosaurus could have run at 34 kilometres per hour on its powerful hind legs.

A a

Ankylosaurus

Pronounced: *an-kyl-oh-sore-uss*

Meaning: **Fused Lizard**. It comes from the Greek **ankýlos**, "bent, crooked or curved" and **sauros**, "lizard."

Ankylosaurus was an armoured dinosaur that lived during the late Cretaceous Period, about 68 to 66 million years ago, in what is now North America.

It lived in forested floodplains and swamps, wooded areas, and lakes where it fed on all types of vegetation and plants.

It weighed around four tonnes and grew to ten metres long and was 1.7 metres tall.

Ankylosaurus's long tail ended in a thick "club" of bone, which it swung as a defence against predators.

The top speed of an Ankylosaurus was not more than ten kilometres per hour. Its life span would have been between seventy and eighty years.

Ankylosaurus had a ridiculously small brain, about the size of a walnut. It was like its close cousin Stegosaurus, the most stupid dinosaur ever!

B b

Brachiosaurus

Pronounced: **Brak-ee-oh-sore-uss**

Meaning: **Arm Lizard**. So named because the front legs were longer than the back legs. From **brachio** and **saurus** "arm-lizard."

Brachiosaurus was a large sauropod that lived 150 million to 130 million years ago from the late Jurassic to the early Cretaceous period in what are now Africa, North America, and Europe.

This giant beast grew to a maximum length of twenty-five metres and a weight of eighty tonnes.

It was built like a huge giraffe with a long neck and short tail.

Brachiosaurus had long, thin, round teeth and unlike most other dinosaurs, it did not chew its food but used its jaws to gather food, which the tongue forced into the throat and was swallowed.

Scientists believe the longer front legs enabled Brachiosaurus to lift its head up to twelve metres above the ground to browse the branches of tall trees.

Brachiosaurus spent its waking hours eating and may have lived up to one hundred years!

C c

Compsognathus

Pronounced: ***Comp-sog-nay-thus***

Meaning: ***Delicate Jaw***. From Greek ***kompos***, "refined, elegant" and ***gnathos***, "jaw."

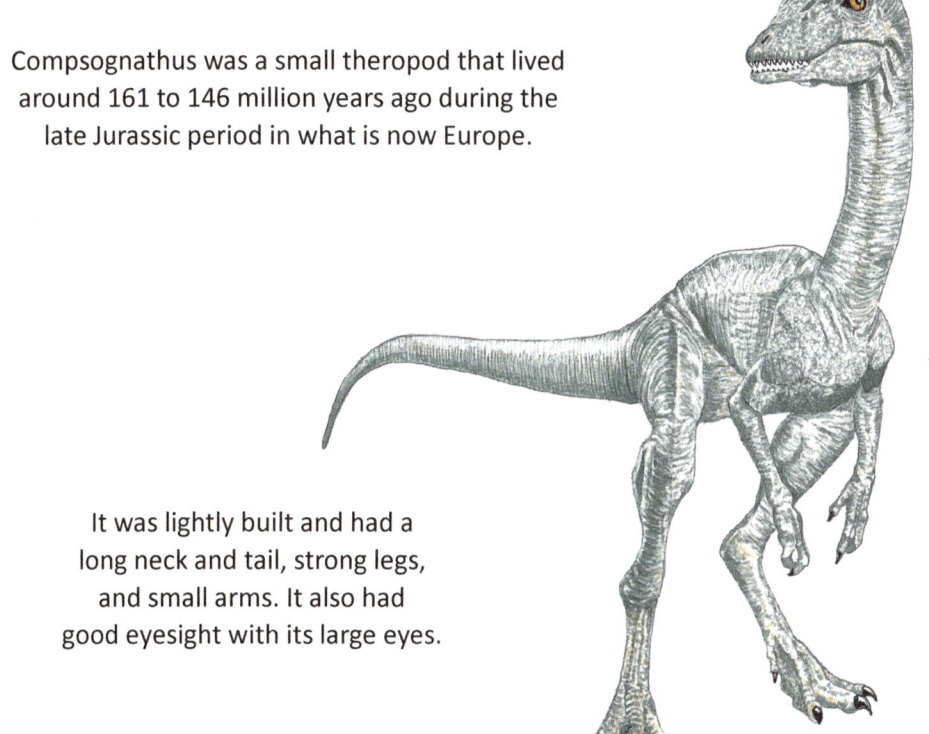

Compsognathus was a small theropod that lived around 161 to 146 million years ago during the late Jurassic period in what is now Europe.

It ate lizards, small mammals, and insects.

Compsognathus was a small dinosaur, so its lifespan is thought to be between five and ten years.

It was lightly built and had a long neck and tail, strong legs, and small arms. It also had good eyesight with its large eyes.

Scientists believe that Compsognathus was a fast mover, it could chase its prey at up to sixty kilometres per hour!

At around sixty to ninety centimetres long, seventy centimetres tall and weighing five kilogrammes, Compsognathus was about the size of a chicken!

D d

Dilophosaurus

Pronounced: **Dai-lo-pho-sore-uss**

Meaning: From the Greek **di,** "two," **lophos** "crest" and **sauros**, "lizard." It gets its name from the two thin crests of bone on the top of its head. It is thought these were used as a display for courtship purposes.

Dilophosaurus was a powerful theropod, one of the largest land animals that lived in what is now North America during the Early Jurassic period, about 201 to 174 million years ago.

Scientists believe that Dilophosaurus may not have been able to hunt down large prey, as the back teeth in the upper jaw were weekly rooted.

It likely that it hunted small or wounded prey, using its large, powerful limbs.

Dilophosaurus was also probably a scavenger, feeding on the carcasses of dead animals.

Scientists also think the design of its teeth would have been ideal for catching fish.

Dilophosaurus was around six metres long and weighed up to 760 kilogrammes.

E e

Edmontosaurus

Pronounced: ***Ed-mon-toe-sore-uss***

Meaning: Edmontosaurus was named from a fossil found in Alberta, Canada. Edmonton is the capital of city Alberta.

Edmontosaurus was a large, duck-billed herbivore from the late Cretaceous period, around seventy-three to sixty-six million years ago, in what is now North America, where it roamed coastal plains.

It had short arms, a long, pointed tail, three-toed, hoofed feet, and mitten-like hands.

Its head was flat and sloping with a wide, toothless beak, cheek pouches, and hundreds of tightly packed cheek teeth that ground up its food.

A fully grown adult could have been thirteen metres in length.

Its weight was around of 4.0 tonnes.

Research suggests that Edmontosaurus could run at high speeds, up to forty-five kilometres per hour!

F f

Fukuiraptor

Pronounced: **Foo-kwee-rap-tor**

Meaning: **Thief of Fukui**. From Japanese **Fukui** and Latin, **raptor** "thief." Fukui is an area of Japan where its fossil was discovered.

Fukuiraptor was a medium-sized theropod that lived during the early Cretaceous period around 127-115 million years ago, in what is now Japan.

It grew to five metres long and 1.5 metres tall. A fully grown adult would have weighed around three hundred kilogrammes.

Fukuiraptor walked on two back legs with three toes on each foot with sharp talons.

It had a long tail that was designed to help it keep balanced while hunting down its prey at speed.

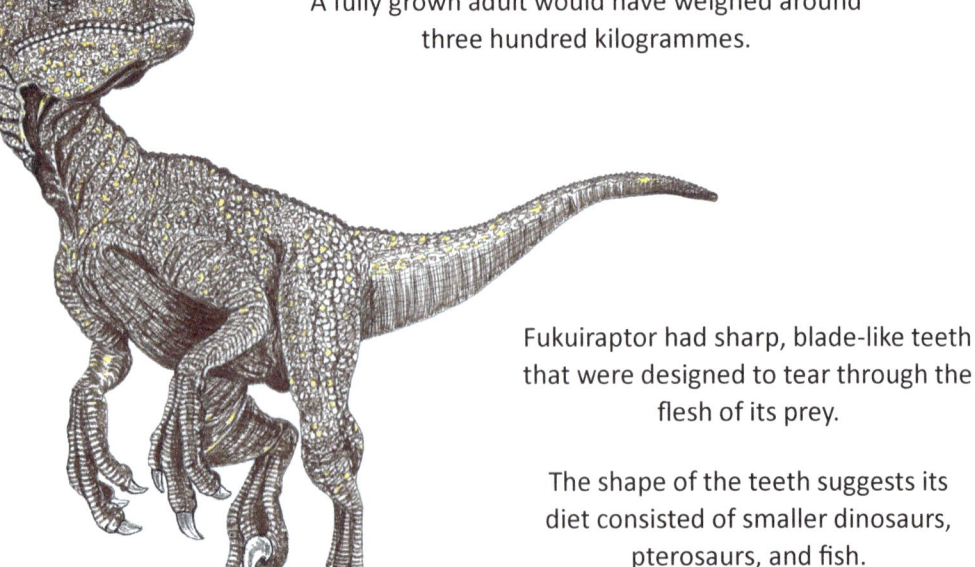

Fukuiraptor had sharp, blade-like teeth that were designed to tear through the flesh of its prey.

The shape of the teeth suggests its diet consisted of smaller dinosaurs, pterosaurs, and fish.

Dilophosaurus was the biggest known predator in its environment and was capable of eating anything it could catch!

G g

Gallimimus

Pronounced: *Gal-uh-my-mus*

Meaning: **Chicken-mimic**. From Latin, **gallus**, "chicken" and **mimus**, "mimic."

Gallimimus was a large ornithomimid theropod that lived during the Late Cretaceous period around seventy million years ago.

It had bird-like features and has been described by researchers as "ostrich-like."

Gallimimus fed on small animals, plants, worms, and insects.

Its mouth was a bird-like beak and was toothless.

It grew to six metres long, stood 2.3 metres tall and weighed up to 440 kilogrammes.

Gallimimus was feathered and had large eyes, remarkably like modern birds. Its legs were incredibly strong, and it could run at speeds up to eighty kilometres per hour!

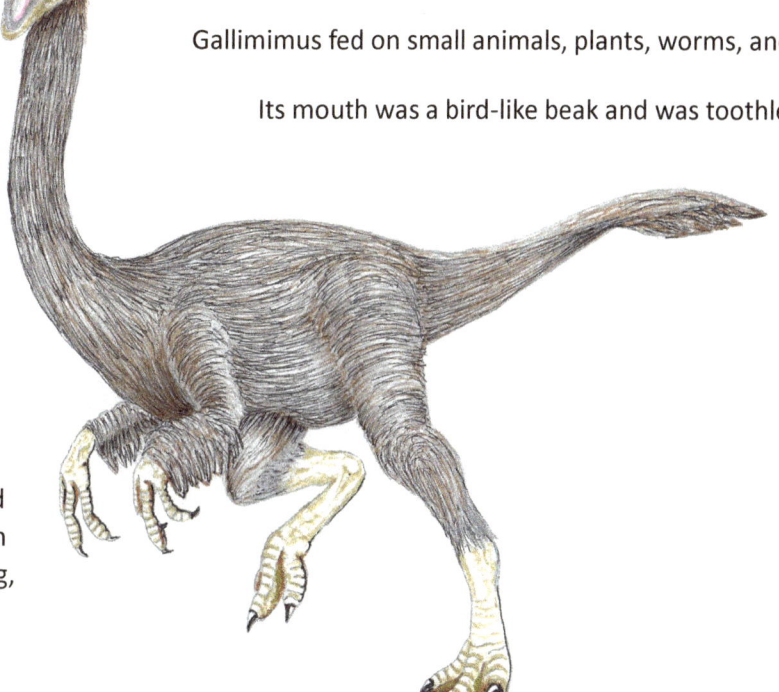

Scientists estimate that unless killed by other predators, Gallimimus could live up to twenty years.

H h

Herrerasaurus

Pronounced: ***Her-rera-sore-uss.***

Meaning: ***Herrera's lizard*** - after the name of the rancher who discovered the first specimen in 1958 in South America.

Herrerasaurus was a theropod that lived during the Late Triassic period, 228 million to two hundred million years ago, in South America.

It had long, powerful hind legs for running and short arms equipped with three curved claws for grasping and tearing. The lower jaw possessed large inward-curving teeth and was flexible for holding prey.

Herrerasaurus reached a length up to 4.5 metres and when fully-grown weighed about 280 kilogrammes.

Researchers believe that this dinosaur lived for around 10-20 years.

Herrerasaurus would search in groups for its prey. It is also known that it ate dead animals as it was an easier way to get food.

Herrerasaurus thrived at a time just before dinosaurs became the dominant land animals.

I i

Iguanodon

Pronounced   *Ig-wana-don*

Meaning: *Iguana Tooth*. From the reptile *Iguana* and Greek *odonys*, "tooth."

Iguanodon was a large herbivore that lived during the Late Jurassic and Early Cretaceous periods, 126 million to 122 million years ago in what are now, Europe, North Africa, North America, Australia, and Asia. It fed on plants, leaves and fruit.

Its skull was small and long. It had a duck-billed mouthful of big, strong, and well-built teeth.

It had a curved neck and a huge body with a fat tail.

Iguanodon spent its time grazing while moving about on four legs, although it was able to walk on two.

Its arm had an unusual five-fingered hand, and the joints of the thumb were fused into a conelike spike; the three middle fingers ended in blunt, hooflike claws; and the fifth finger stuck out from the others.

Iguanodon weighed around four tonnes and was nine metres long.

For self-defence, it had sharp thumb spikes and fingernails

Iguanodon species lived in large groups in forests and plains.

If it managed to avoid being eaten by a carnivore, Iguanodon had an average lifespan of around 25 years.

J j
Juravenator

Pronounced;   *ju-rah-ve-nay-tor*

Meaning: A hunter from the **Jura** mountains in Germany. **Venator** is the Latin for "hunter"

Juravenator was a small theropod carnivore that lived during the late Jurassic period, 154 to 151 million years ago in what is now Germany.

It hunted in forests, floodplains, swamps, riversides and fed on fish, birds, and any small animal it could catch.

Juravenator grew to a length of seventy-five centimetres and weighed up to five hundred grammes.

It was a small dinosaur with a lean body and rounded belly. The skull was narrow and elongated. The skin was bumpy and pebble-like. It may have had feathers.

The exact speed of Juravenator is unknown, but it is thought to be a fast and ferocious predator!

Scientists believe Juravenator to have had a life span of up 30 years.

K k

Khaan

Pronounced: **_Karn_**

The name means: **_Ruler_**. From the Mongolian word for "Emperor" or "Ruler."

Khaan was a small oviraptorid theropod which lived during the Late Cretaceous period, 81-75 million years ago in what is now Mongolia.

It was about 1.2 metres long and weighed up to thirteen kilogrammes.

Khaan was known to be partially carnivorous, feeding on small mammals, lizards, and small dinosaurs as well as roots, insects, and worms.

Its upper and lower jaws were toothless, and it had a powerful beak for feeding.

It had large claws on its feet used for digging and defence.

Khaan could chase its prey at speeds up to sixty kilometres per hour!

L l

Leptoceratops

Pronounced: **Lehp-toe-sehr-ah-tops**

Meaning: **Slender horned face** From Greek **lepto**," small," **kerat**, "horn" and **ops**, "face."

Leptoceratops was a ceratopsian herbivore that lived during the Late Cretaceous period, sixty-seven to sixty-five million years ago in what is now North America.

It lived in flatlands, forests, deserts, beaches, woodlands and wetlands, areas with plentiful vegetation, where it fed on plants including ferns, cycads, and conifers.

Leptoceratops weighed up to two hundred kilogrammes and stood around 0.8 metres tall with a body length of around 2.75 metres.

Strangely, although the dinosaur's name means slender horned face, it did not have horns!

M m

Megalosaurus

Pronounced: **Meg-al-oh-sore-uss**

Meaning: **Great Lizard**. From Greek **megas**, "great" and **sauros**, "lizard."

It could run at about thirty kilometres per hour.

Megalosaurus was a large theropod that lived during the Late Jurassic period, 176-161 million years ago, in what are now England and Africa.

It had a thick, strong neck and a large head. Its jaws were strong and had curved, sharp, and dagger-like teeth.

The arms of the Megalosaurus were short and strong. Fingers on the arms were clawed and grasping and worked like hands. The legs were muscular and long and had claws on three toes of both feet. The tail was thick and long.

The dinosaur was around six metres long and three metres tall.

The average weight of a full-grown adult was around 820 kilogrammes.

Megalosaurus was a vicious predator which ate other dinosaurs like Sauropods and Stegosaurs, insects, lizards, and early mammals. It is believed to be the first dinosaur ever described scientifically.

British fossil hunter William Buckland named Megalosaurus in 1824.

N n
Nasutoceratops

Pronounced: **Na-su-to-seh-ra-tops.**

Meaning: **Big-nose-horn-face**. From Latin **nasutus**, "large-nosed," and **ceratops**, "horned-face."

It lived in flatlands and forest areas where it fed on fruits, seeds, leaves, twigs, and roots.

Nasutoceratops was a medium-sized ceratopsian herbivore that lived during the Late Cretaceous period, eighty-three to seventy million years ago in what is now North America.

Nasutoceratops was known for its short-snout and one-metre-long horns that curved over the eyes, like the ones that we see on modern-day cattle.

Nasutoceratops weighed around 2.25 tonnes and stood 1.5 metres tall and was 4.5 metres long.

The length of the skull was about one and a half metres

The speed of Nasutoceratops is currently unknown, however, it can be estimated through their build, that these dinosaurs were slow movers as they had a large body mass.

O o

Ouranosaurus

Pronounced: *Aou-rae-noe-sore-uss.*

Meaning: **Brave lizard**. From the Arabic word for "courage" and Greek, *sauros*, "lizard."

Ouranosaurus was a large herbivore that lived in the Early Cretaceous period, 115-100 million years ago in what is now Africa.

It lived on vast plains, in forests, and on the tundra – although the tundra had little food to support plant and animal life.

It would have fed on any vegetation, plants, and roots it could find.

Ouranosaurus was a large beast weighing in at five tonnes, standing 5.5 metres tall with a body length exceeding seven metres.

It is thought that if in danger it could run at a speeds up to forty kilometres per hour.

Scientists think that this animal could have lived for about 50 years.

P p

Pachycephalosaurus

Pronounced: **Pak-ee-seph-al-oh-sore-uss**

Meaning: **Thick-headed Lizard**. From Greek **pachys**, "thick," **kephale**, "head" and **sauros**, "lizard"

Pachycephalosaurus was the largest of the bone-headed herbivores. It lived during the Late Cretaceous period, seventy-six to sixty-six million years ago in what is what is now North America.

It grazed in forests and on flatlands feeding on plants, leaves, fruits, and vegetables.

Pachycephalosaurus weighed 450 kilogrammes when fully grown and grew to a length of four and a half metres.

Its height can be compared to that of a full-grown cow or buffalo.

It had small teeth and a mouth like a beak. The skull was small and round. Its eyes were large and its nose, small.

Pachycephalosaurus moved on its hindlegs, which were big and strong.

The forearms were small, and It had a long fat tail.

The bone protecting its brain, which also had spikes around it, was at least twenty times thicker than that of other dinosaurs!

P p

Parasaurolophus

Pronounced: *Para-sore-oh-loph-uss.*

Meaning: *Near crested lizard*. From Greek *para*, "beside" or "near" *sauros*, and *lophos*, "crest"

Parasaurolophos was a large herbivore that lived during the Late Cretaceous period, seventy-six to seventy-three million years ago in what are now Asia and North America.

It moved on all-fours when foraging but ran on its hind legs.

Scientists believe Parasaurolophos was a strong swimmer and may have used this skill to get away from predators, by escaping into water.

An adult weighed up to three tonnes and grew to a length of eleven metres and stood 2.7 metres tall.

It is believed that Parasaurolophus could run at speeds up to forty kilometres per hour.

Scientists also believe that the crest was more than just decorative but was used to produce a unique sound for communication.

Q q
Quilmesaurus

Pronounced: ***Kwil-me-sore-uss***

Meaning: The name **Quilmesaurus** comes from the name of a local tribe of native Americans, **Quilmes**, who live in the region where the fossils were found and Greek *sauros*, "lizard."

Quilmesaurus was a theropod that lived during the Late Cretaceous period, seventy-five to sixty-six million years ago, in what is now South America.

It roamed woodlands, grasslands, and forests, with plentiful vegetation in which to find its prey which included, pterosaurs, small theropods and herbivores.

An adult Quilmesaurus grew to around five metres in length stood 1,75 metres tall and weighed in at 450 kilogrammes.

Scientists estimate that although there is no firm evidence of speed, considering the length of its leg and the size of its body, Quilmesaurus was a fast mover.

R r

Rugops

Pronounced: **Roo-gops**

Meaning: ***Wrinkled face***. From Latin ***rugosa***, "wrinkle" and Greek ***ops***, 'face'.

Rugops was a theropod that lived during the Late Cretaceous period, ninety-five million years ago in what is now Africa.

It had a delicate skull which suggests it was a scavenger and not an attacking dinosaur like tyrannosaurs and raptors.

Scientists estimate the size of Rugops to have been around four metres in length, standing 1.5 metres tall and weighing up to five hundred kilogrammes.

Scientists estimate that Rugops could run as fast as forty kilometres per hour.

Rows of holes in the skull indicate that it may have had a crest of some kind.

Rugops had truly short arms that were useless for defence but functioned as a counter-balance.

S s

Spinosaurus

Pronounced: ***Spy-no-sore-uss***

Meaning: ***Sail-back***. From Latin ***spina***, "a thorn, prickle or spine" and Greek ***sauros***, "lizard."

Spinosaurus was a huge theropod that lived during the late Cretaceous period, ninety-five to seventy million years ago in what is now North Africa.

It is the largest carnivorous dinosaur yet to be discovered.

It grew to eighteen metres long and weighed in at around sixteen tonnes.

Its skull alone was 1.75 metres in length, longer than the average person.

The skull was long and narrow and unlike other theropods its nostrils were close to its eyes and not at the end of the snout. The snout has many small pits. These are thought to have housed pressure sensors to detect prey in murky waters, as those in living crocodiles today.

Spinosaurus' teeth were straight and cone-shaped unlike the curved serrated teeth of most other theropods. Its most distinctive feature was the huge sail that rose from its back to a height of two metres.

The sail bones were part of the spine.

Having the nostrils close to the eyes meant that it could breathe whilst keeping its snout full of huge teeth underwater waiting to ambush its prey.

Not a great deal is known about Spinosaurus, but scientists believe it may have spent a lot of time in water and that its main diet would have been large prehistoric fish and reptiles.

S s

Stegosaurus

Pronounced: **Steg-ah-sore-uss.**

Meaning: ***Roofed-lizard***, which came from the belief by 19th-century paleontologists that the back-plates lay flat along its spine, like the tiles on a roof. From Greek ***stegos***, "a roof" and ***saurus***, "lizard."

Stegosaurus was a large herbivore which lived during the Late Jurassic period, 159 million to 144 million years ago, in what are now North America, Africa, China, and Europe.

The skull and brain were exceedingly small for such a large animal, the brain was about half the size of a sheep's brain!

Its front legs were much shorter than its back legs, which gave the back an arched appearance.

The feet were short and broad.

Stegosaurus usually grew to a length of about 6.5 metres, but some reached nine metres

A fully grown adult could weigh eight tonnes!

It had a spiked tail which it used to defend itself from predators such as the Allosaurus.

However, the huge back plates called scutes may not have been used as armour but as an appealing feature to attract mates.

If it was not eaten by an Allosaurus, Stegosaurus may have lived up to one hundred years!

T t

Triceratops

Pronounced: *Tri- sehr-ah-tops*

Meaning: **Three-horn-face.** from the Greek words **trí**, "three", **kéras** "horn", and **ops**, "face".

Triceratops lived during the Late Cretaceous period around sixty-eight to sixty-six million years ago, in what is now North America.

This horned dinosaur inhabited forest areas, marsh ranges, and plains with dense vegetation.

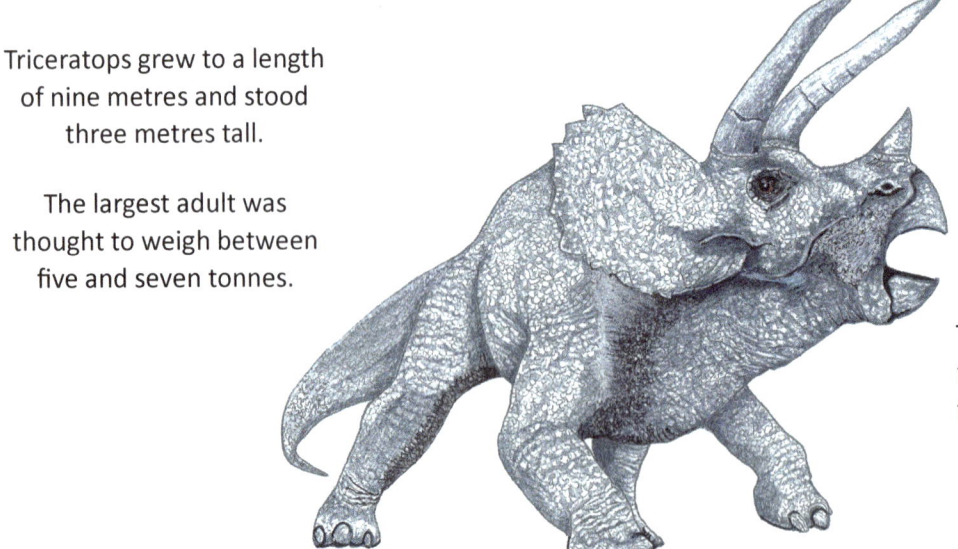

Triceratops grew to a length of nine metres and stood three metres tall.

The largest adult was thought to weigh between five and seven tonnes.

These dinosaurs are known for their heavy body and the large frill that served the purpose of defence against larger predators and was used by males to attract mates.

The large neck frill and its heavy head were in some cases, almost one-third of the size of its entire body.

Scientists believe that the two horns on the head of the dinosaur were made of bones and the third horn was made up of keratin. The human fingernail is also made up of keratin.

T t

Tyrannosaurus Rex

Pronounced: **Tuh-ran-uh-sore-uss-rex**

Meaning: **Tyrant lizard king. Tyrannosaurus** is Greek for "tyrant lizard," and **Rex** means "king" in Latin.

T-Rex lived during the Cretaceous period, sixty-eight to sixty-six million years ago in what is now North America.

This fearsome predator roamed coastal swamps, open forests, and tropical regions where it preyed on smaller dinosaurs, although scientists believe it also hunted and killed the larger Triceratops.

It had short arms with only two fingers that could barely reach its mouth!

Despite having powerful legs, T-Rex was not a fast mover. It could not travel at more than five kilometres per hour.

It was a huge beast, growing to twelve metres in length, standing four metres tall and weighing up to eight tonnes!

It had sixty serrated teeth the longest of which was thirty centimetres in length.

Its skull alone was 1.5 metres long!

T rex could fit as much as 285 kilogrammes of food in its mouth per bite.

Based on growth rings in fossil bones, scientists know that the longest-lived T-Rex so far discovered died at the age of twenty-eight years. It had suffered many injuries over its short life.

U u

Utahraptor

Pronounced: *You-tah-wrap-terr.*

Meaning: From **Utah**, the American state where its fossil was discovered, and Latin **raptor**, "plunderer, or "robber".

Utahraptor was the largest of all raptor dinosaurs. It was also the oldest of this family. It lived 129 to 122 million years ago, during the Early Cretaceous period in what is now North America, where it hunted smaller dinosaurs and mammals in floodplains and forests.

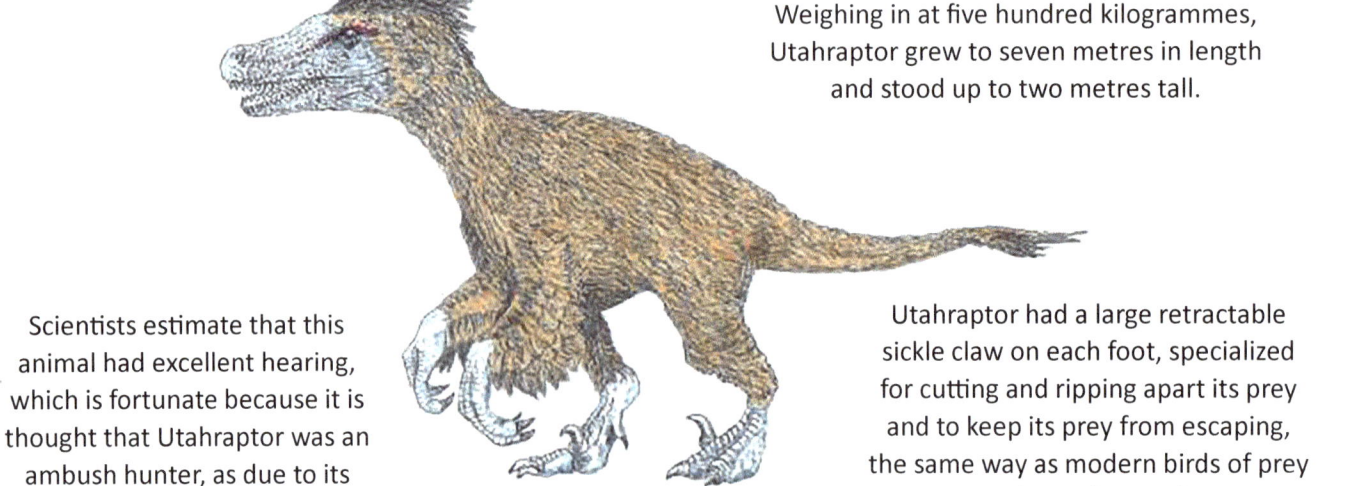

Weighing in at five hundred kilogrammes, Utahraptor grew to seven metres in length and stood up to two metres tall.

Scientists estimate that this animal had excellent hearing, which is fortunate because it is thought that Utahraptor was an ambush hunter, as due to its enormous size and weight, it was incapable of running fast!

Utahraptor had a large retractable sickle claw on each foot, specialized for cutting and ripping apart its prey and to keep its prey from escaping, the same way as modern birds of prey use their talons today.

The claw itself was twenty-four centimetres long!

Although Utahraptor resembled birds through its flimsy feathers, there is no certain evidence that it would have evolved into a modern bird species.

It is certain that Utahraptor could not fly!

V v

Velociraptor

Pronounced: ***Vel-oss-ee-rap-tor***

Meaning: ***Quick Thief***. From Latin ***velox***, "swift" and ***raptor***, "robber, plunderer"

Velociraptor was a theropod that roamed the Earth during the Late Cretaceous period, seventy-four to seventy million years ago in what are now Mongolia and China. It lived in hot and dry regions, where it preyed upon small dinosaurs, reptiles, insects, mammals, and amphibians.

Velociraptor weighed around fifteen kilogrammes, was two metres long and stood half a metre tall.

It had a large skull, long snout, sharp teeth, and a small body with a stiff tail.

The jaws were provided with 26-28 teeth on each side, which were spaced out widely and jagged.

The lifespan of a Velociraptor is estimated to have been about fifteen to twenty years.

Noticeable features of the Velociraptor are two large hands, each of which has three curved claws. The second toe of each foot was paired with a sickle-shaped and sharp talon.

The use of these talons was to keep its prey from escaping, the same way modern birds of prey use their talons.

As with other members of the raptor family although it was a feathered dinosaur, it could not fly.

W w

Wendiceratops

Pronounced: ***Wendy- sehr-ah-tops***

Meaning: ***Wendy's horned-face*** in honour of well-known Alberta fossil hunter Wendy Sloboda. From ***Wendy***, Greek, ***keras***, "horn," and ***ops***, "face."

Wendiceratops was a herbivore that lived during the Late Cretaceous period, eighty-two to seventy-two million years ago, in what is now North America. It would crop low-lying plants with a parrot-like beak and slice them up with dozens of leaf-shaped teeth.

Wendiceratops grew to six metres long, stood about 2.5 metres at the centre of its arched back and weighed around one tonne.

It had a group of thorn-like structures sticking out along the edge of its broad frill. This frill was a unique, broad shield-shaped structure with its base attached to the rear side of its head.

The short, stumpy nose horn stood upright and was around eight centimetres tall. It also had brow horns above the eye sockets.

Wendiceratops is a relative of the famous Triceratops. Like its famous cousin, it has a rhino-like body and moved on four legs.

X x

Xiongguanlong

Pronounced: ***Zhong-gwan-long***

Meaning: ***Dragon from Xiong Guan***, or "Grand Pass dragon" from Chinese.

Xiongguanlong was a theropod that lived about 125-100 million years ago during the Early Cretaceous period in what is now China.

It was a member of the Tyrannosaur family.

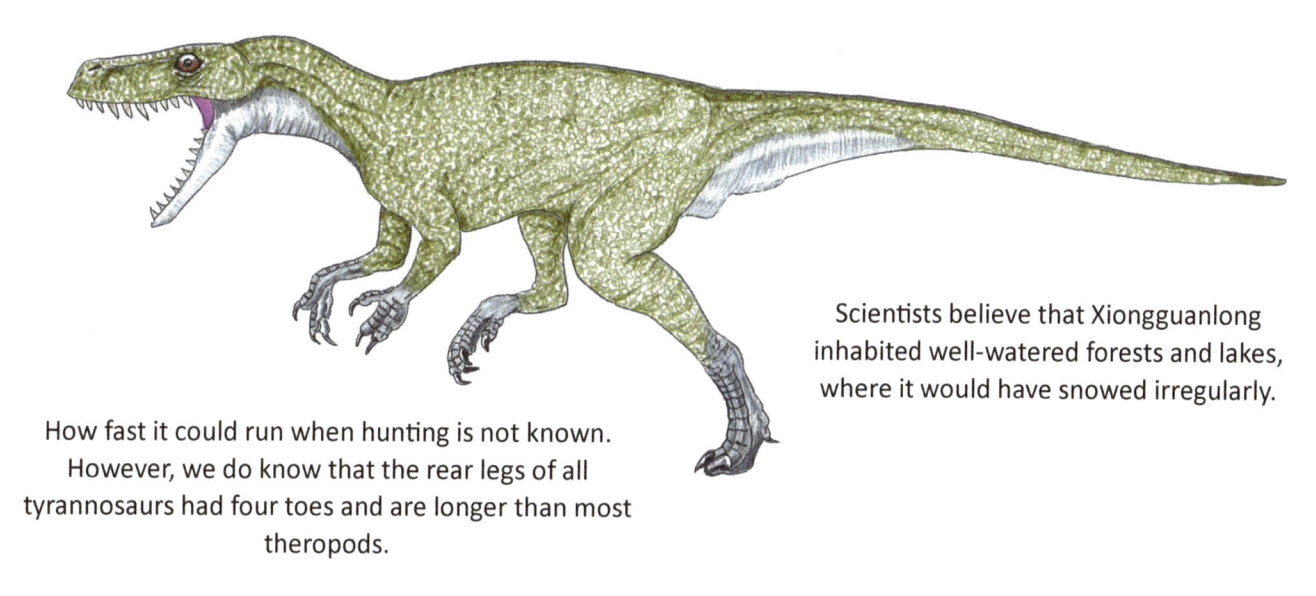

Scientists believe that Xiongguanlong inhabited well-watered forests and lakes, where it would have snowed irregularly.

How fast it could run when hunting is not known. However, we do know that the rear legs of all tyrannosaurs had four toes and are longer than most theropods.

This suggests that smaller tyrannosaurs like Xiongguanlong were fast runners. It is believed that like most theropods they moved on their hind legs.

Xiongguanlong grew up to 3.6 in length, 1,5 metres tall at the hip and weighed up to 270 kilogrammes.

Like all other tyrannosaurs, it preyed on small and medium-sized animals.

Y y
Yutyrannous

Pronounced: *Yu-tee-ran-uss*

Meaning: **Feathered Tyrant**. From Mandarin Chinese **Yu**, "feather" and Latinised Greek **tyrannos** "tyrant".

Yutyrannus was a theropod tyrannosaur that lived during the Early Cretaceous period, 145 million years ago, in what is now China.

It fed on small animals and other dinosaurs like sauropods.

Yutyrannus weighed around 1.4 tonnes, was nine metres long and stood up to five metres tall.

Despite its size, the Yutyrannus could run at speeds of fifty to sixty kilometres per hour!

Palaeontologists discovered that this dinosaur was covered in an early type of feathers that formed a downy cover on its body to keep it warm.

It is thought that Yutyrannous inhabited well-watered forests and lakes, where it often snowed.

It is currently the largest dinosaur to provide direct evidence of feathers on dinosaurs.

Z z

Zephyrosaurus

Pronounced: *Zef-e-ir-sore-us*

Meaning: ***Westward Wind Lizard***. from Greek mythology, the Greek god of the west wind, ***Zephyros***, and ***saurus***, "lizard"

Zephyrosaurus was a herbivore that lived during the Early Cretaceous period, 120 to 110 million years ago in what is now North America.

It lived in forests, plains, deserts, shorelines, and wetlands.

Zephyrosaurus had a prominent beak and sharp teeth. It had long feet that almost resemble those of a kangaroo.

The shape of the feet suggests that this dinosaur could jump and hop around easily.

It was 1.8 m long and ninety centimetres tall.

Scientists believe that Zephyrosaurus was an agile, fast runner.

Scientists believe that Zephyrosaurus was a burrowing animal which means it dug the earth to find food.

The typical Zephyrosaurus diet primarily consisted of plants and seeds.

Glossary

Amphibian

A cold-blooded vertebrate animal of a class that comprises the frogs, toads, newts, and salamanders.

Ankylosaurs

Herbivorous dinosaurs from the Cretaceous Period, having the body covered with thick, bony plates.

Aquatic

Growing or living in or visiting water

Avian

Relating to or coming from birds. Avian dinosaurs were reliant on flight, and therefore their bones developed to allow them to fly.

Biology

Biology is the scientific study of life.

Bipedal

An animal using only two feet for walking

Carnivores

Animals feeding on other animals.

Ceratopsian

Four-footed, herbivorous dinosaurs of the late Cretaceous Period, having an enlarged skull with a beak, a large, perforated frill at the back. Some species, one or three horns. Also called horned dinosaur.

Cretaceous

The Cretaceous is a geological period that lasted from about 145 to 66 million years ago. It is the third and final period of the Mesozoic Era.

Dinosaur

Dinosaurs were the main animals on Earth for more than 150 million years. They were lizard like reptiles. Some of them were the largest creatures that ever walked on land. The word dinosaur comes from Greek words meaning "terrible lizard." The last dinosaurs became extinct, or died out, about sixty-six million years ago.

Fossil

Fossils are the preserved remains, or traces of remains, of ancient animals or plants. Fossils are not the remains of the organism itself! They are rocks. A fossil can preserve an entire organism or just part of one

Geological

Relating to the study of the earth's physical structure and substance.

Gondwana

One of the two ancient supercontinents produced by the first split of the even larger supercontinent Pangaea about two hundred million years ago, comprising chiefly what are now Africa, South America, Australia, Antarctica, and the Indian subcontinent.

Herbivores

Animals that feed on plants.

Ichthyosaur

A marine reptile of the Mesozoic era, resembling a dolphin with a long-pointed head, four flippers, and a vertical tail.

Jurassic

The period of the Mesozoic era between the Triassic and the Cretaceous (201 – 145 million years ago), marked by the presence of dinosaurs and the first appearance of birds.

K/T Extinction

A global extinction event responsible for eliminating approximately 80 percent of all species of animals at or close to the boundary between the Cretaceous and Paleogene periods, about sixty-six million years ago.

Laurasia

One of the two ancient supercontinents produced by the first split of the even larger supercontinent Pangaea about two hundred million years ago, comprising what are now North America, Greenland, Europe, and Asia

Mass Extinction Event

A mass extinction event is when species vanish faster than they are replaced. This is usually defined as about 75% of the world's species being lost in a 'short' amount of geological time - less than 2.8 million years.

Mesozoic

Mesozoic (252-66 million years ago) means 'middle life', and this is the time of the dinosaurs. This era includes the Triassic, Jurassic, and Cretaceous Periods.

Mosasaurs

A group of extinct, large marine reptiles from the Late Cretaceous Period.

Non-avian Dinosaurs

Avian and non-avian dinosaurs had different ways of converting food into energy and the non-avian dinosaurs were cold-blooded, more like reptiles, while the avian dinosaurs were warm-blooded, more like mammals.

Ornithomimids

Lightly built medium-sized dinosaurs having extremely long limbs and necks with small heads and big brains and large eyes, just like an Ostrich.

Palaeontology

Palaeontology is the study of prehistoric life forms (or fossils) preserved in rocks and ancient sediments and the evolution of life on Earth. It involves not only geology but also aspects of biology and chemistry.

Palaeontologist

Someone who studies fossils as a way of getting information about the history of life on Earth

Pangea

Pangea, also spelled Pangaea, was a supercontinent that incorporated all the landmasses on Earth.

Panthalassa

The super-ocean that surrounded the supercontinent Pangaea,

Permian

The Permian period, which ended in the largest mass extinction the Earth has ever known, began about 299 million years ago.

Plesiosaur

A large marine reptile of the Mesozoic era, with a broad flat body, large paddle-like limbs, and typically a long flexible neck and small head. Plesiosaurs ranged in length from less than 2 metres to more than seventeen metres. The name means 'Almost-lizard.'

Pliosaurs

Pliosaurs (meaning "more lizard") are another group of Jurassic marine reptiles. Unlike their long-necked plesiosaur cousins, these animals had short necks with a large, elongated head like crocodiles. Pliosaurs ranged from around four to ten metres in length but could be up to fifteen metres. Pliosaurs also had two pairs of powerful paddles and a short tail.

Prehistoric

The period before written records.

Pterosaurs

From the size of a sparrow to the size of an airplane, the pterosaurs (Greek for "wing lizards") flew the skies in the Jurassic and Cretaceous Periods, and included the largest vertebrate ever known to fly: the late Cretaceous Quetzalcoatlus.

Sauropod

Meaning 'Lizard-footed' - dinosaur, marked by enormous size, a long neck and tail, a four-legged stance, and a herbivorous diet. These reptiles were the largest of all dinosaurs and the largest land animals that ever lived.

Theropod

Meaning 'Beast-footed' - includes all the flesh-eating dinosaurs. Theropods were the most diverse group of saurischian ("lizard-hipped") dinosaurs,

Triassic

The Triassic Period was the first period of the Mesozoic Era. It began 252 million years ago, at the close of the Permian Period, and ended 201 million years ago, when it was succeeded by the Jurassic Period.

Vertebrate

Vertebrates are life-forms which have interlocking bones that form the spinal column, also called vertebrae. They have a hard skeleton made of bone, which supports the body's tissue and anchor muscle. Animals that do not have spines are called invertebrates.

Lightning Source UK Ltd.
Milton Keynes UK
UKHW050730261122
412824UK00009B/119